2 to 22 DAYS IN GREAT BRITAIN

THE ITINERARY PLANNER

1991 Edition

RICK STEVES

John Muir Publications
Santa Fe, New Mexico

Originally published as *22 Days in Great Britain*.

Thanks to my eternal travel partner, research assistant, and wife, Anne. Thanks also to Roy Nichols and Dave Hoerlein for their research help, to our well-traveled readers for their input, and the British friends listed in this book who make a visit there so much more than a series of palaces, museums, and Big Bens.

John Muir Publications, P.O. Box 613, Santa Fe, NM 87504

1991 Edition

Library of Congress Cataloging-in-Publication Data
Steves, Rick, 1955-
    2 to 22 days in Great Britain : the itinerary planner / Rick
Steves. — 1991 ed.
        p.   cm.
    Rev. ed. of: 22 days in Great Britain. 3rd ed. 1989.
    Includes index.
    ISBN 0-945465-85-8
    1. Great Britain—Description and travel—1971- —Tours.
I. Steves, Rick, 1955-   22 days in Great Britain. II. Title.
III. Title: Two to twenty-two days in Great Britain.
DA650.S75 1991
914.104'858—dc20   91-7563
                                                            CIP

Distributed to the book trade by
W.W. Norton & Company, Inc.
New York, New York

Maps   Dave Hoerlein
Cover   Jennifer Dewey
Typography   Copygraphics, Inc., Santa Fe, NM
Printer   McNaughton & Gunn, Inc.

CONTENTS

How to Use this Book   1
Back Door Travel Philosophy   21
Itinerary   22
Day 1   Fly to London   27
Days 2 and 3 The Best of London   43
Day 4   Salisbury, Stonehenge, Bath   56
Day 5   Bath, England's Cover-Girl Town   60
Day 6   Wells, Glastonbury, Wookey Hole   66
Day 7   South Wales, Folk Musuem, Wye River Valley   69
Day 8   The Cotswold Villages and Blenheim Palace   74
Day 9   Stratford-upon-Avon, Warwick Castle, and Coventry Cathedral to Ironbridge Gorge   79
Day 10   Ironbridge Gorge Museums—North Wales   84
Day 11   Exploring North Wales   91
Day 12   Blackpool, England's Coney Island   95
Day 13   The Windermere Lake District   100
Day 14   Exploring the Lake District   106
Day 15   Lake District to the West Coast of Scotland   109
Day 16   Highlands, Loch Ness, Scenic Drive   113
Day 17   Edinburgh   117
Day 18   Edinburgh   124
Day 19   Edinburgh—Hadrian's Wall—Durham   130
Day 20   North York Moors and York   136
Day 21   York   141
Day 22   York—Cambridge—London   144
Posttour Option: Ireland   150
Appendix
22 Days in Great Britain by Train and Bus   156
What's So Great About Britain?   161
Telephone Directory   169
Weights and Measures   170
British-Yankee Vocabulary   171
Index   173

GREAT BRITAIN

LEWIS
SKYE
LOCH NESS
FINDHORN
INVERNESS
HIGHLANDS
BEN NEVIS
PITLOCHRY
MULL
OBAN
SCOTLAND
EDINBURGH
GLASGOW
BORDERS
HADRIAN'S WALL
N. IRE.
BELFAST
LAKE DIST.
DURHAM
STAITHES
WHITBY
ISLE OF MAN
MOORS
YORK
IRELAND
BLACKPOOL
DUBLIN
LIVERPOOL
ENGLAND
SNOWDONIA NAT'L. PARK
CHESTER
RUTHIN
IRON BRIDGE
COVENTRY
ELY
WALES
WARWICK
CAMBRIDGE
STRATFORD
STOW
COTSWOLDS
TINTERN
LONDON ★
GOWER PEN.
CARDIFF
BATH
DOVER
WELLS
STONEHENGE
CALAIS
GLASTONBURY
SALISBURY
BOULOGNE
CORNWALL
ENGLISH CHANNEL
FRANCE
DIEPPE

0   50   100
MILES

DCH

HOW TO USE THIS BOOK

This book organizes Britain into an efficient, enjoyable, and diverse 22-day adventure. It's the tour guide in your pocket. It lets you be the boss by giving you the best 2,000 miles and 22 days in Britain and a suggested way to use that time most efficiently.

2 to 22 Days in Great Britain is for do-it-yourselfers who would like the organization and smoothness of a tour without the straitjacket. It's having your cake and eating it, too. This plan is maximum thrills per mile, minute, and dollar. It's designed for travel by rental car but adaptable to train (see train schedule in the Appendix). The pace is fast but not hectic and is designed for the American with limited time who wants to see everything but doesn't want the "if it's Tuesday this must be Edinburgh" craziness. The plan includes the predictable "required" biggies (such as Big Ben, Stratford, Wordsworth's cottage, and Stonehenge) with a good dose of "Back Door" intimacy—cozy Cotswold villages, windswept Roman lookouts, Gaelic folk pubs, angelic boys' choirs—mixed in.

2 to 22 Days in Great Britain is balanced and streamlined, reducing the chance of typical tourist burnout by including only the most exciting castles and churches. I've been very selective. For example, we won't visit both Oxford and Cambridge—just the better of the two. Which is better is, of course, only my opinion. But after 12 busy years of travel writing, lecturing, and tour guiding, I've developed a sixth sense for what tickles the traveler's fancy. I love this itinerary. I get excited just thinking about it.

Of course, connect-the-dots travel isn't perfect, just as color-by-number painting isn't good art. But this book is your smiling Scotsman, your Bobbie in a bind, your handbook. It's your well thought out and tested itinerary. I've done it—and refined it—many times on my own and with groups. Use it, take advantage of it, but don't let it rule you.

Read this book before you begin your trip. Use it as a rack to hang more ideas on. As you plan and study and travel and talk to people, you'll fill the margins with notes. It's your tool. The book is flexible, with 22 re-arrangeable units (days), each built with these sections:

1. **Introductory overview** for the day.

2. An hour-by-hour **Suggested Schedule** recommended for that day.

3. List of the most important **Sightseeing Highlights** rated: ▲▲▲ Don't miss; ▲▲ Try hard to see; ▲ Worthwhile if you can make it; (no rating) Worth knowing about.

4. **Transportation** tips and instructions.

5. **Food and Accommodations**: How and where to find the best budget places, including addresses, phone numbers, and my favorites.

6. **Orientation** and an easy-to-read map locating all recommended places.

7. **Helpful Hints** on shopping, transportation, day-to-day chores.

8. **Itinerary Options** for those with more or less than the suggested time, or with particular interests. This itinerary is rubbery!

Dave Hoerlein knows a good map is worth a thousand words. His maps make my text easy to follow. Dave points out all major landmarks, streets, and accommodations mentioned in the book and indicates the best city entry and exit routes for our 22-day plan. His maps are clear, concise, and readable but are designed to only orient and direct you until you pick up something better at the tourist information office.

At the end of the book, you'll find special sections on such things as English history and politics and Ireland, as well as train schedules and a telephone directory.

Cost

This trip's cost breaks down like this: a basic round-trip U.S.A.-London flight, $600-$1,000 (depending on the season and where you fly from); a three-week car rental (split between two people, including tax, insurance, and gas) or three weeks of rail and bus travel, $400; for room and board, figure $50 a day, double occupancy, for a total of $1,100 per person. This is more than feasible, and if necessary, you can travel cheaper (see my book *Europe Through the Back Door*, Santa Fe, N.M.: John Muir Publications, 1990, for the skills, tricks, and thrills of traveling cheap). Add $200 or $300 fun money and you've got yourself a great British adventure for around $2,600.

This Book's Price Rating System
Because exact prices are impossible to predict, most prices in this book are given according to these general ratings:

Accommodations: 1991 price per person in a double room with a full English breakfast unless otherwise noted:

cheap	inexpensive	moderate	expensive
under £13	£13-17	£17-23	over £23
under $26	$26-34	$34-46	over $46

Although B&Bs usually have a straight per-person price, some (and most hotels) have more expensive singles and less expensive triples and quads. Showers are readily available but almost always down the hall. Remember, "expensive" in this book is "budget" in most other guidebooks.

Meals: 1991 price for a three-course meal, which includes soup or salad, meat, vegetables, dessert, service, but not drinks (add $2 for a large beer and $1 for coffee, tea, or soft drinks; water is always free):

cheap	inexpensive	moderate	expensive
under £4	£4-6	£6-10	over £10
under $8	$8-12	$12-20	over $20

Prices and Times
I've priced things in pounds (£) throughout the book. I haven't cluttered this book with many minor prices (such as specific admission fees and student discounts). Small charges of less than a dollar shouldn't affect your sight-seeing decisions. Prices, as well as hours, telephone num-

bers, and so on, are accurate as of late 1990. Exchange
rates are always changing, and I've tossed timidity out the
window, knowing you'll understand that this book, like
any guidebook, starts to yellow before it's even printed.
Britain sticks to its schedule (pronounced "shed-jool")
better than most European countries, but do what you
can to double-check hours and times when you arrive.
The hours listed are for peak season. Many places close
an hour earlier in the off-season. Some are open only on
weekends or are closed entirely in the winter. Confirm
your sightseeing plans locally—especially when traveling
between October and May. Many sights shift into winter
schedules, closing earlier when daylight savings time is
over in late October.

Money
The British pound sterling (£) is broken into 100 pence
(p). A pound or "quid" is worth about $2.00. Pence
means "cents." You'll find coins ranging from 5 pence to
£1 and bills from £5 to £50.

To figure pounds into dollars, multiply the British
prices by two. For example, £6 = $12, £4.50 = $9, and
80p = $1.60. Get used to this formula as soon as possible.
(The actual exchange rate floats. Whether its 1.92 or 2.08,
just keep it simple and go with your rough estimates.)

Scotland and Ireland have their own currencies. English and Scottish money are worth the same and are good
in both countries (but it can be troublesome to spend
Scottish currency in England). The Irish-English money
relationship is like the Canadian-American one. English
money is a little more valuable. Ireland is a different
country—treat it that way.

Britain's 15 percent sales tax, the "value added tax," or
"VAT," is built into nearly everything you buy. Tourists
can get a refund on this VAT on souvenirs they take out of
the country, but it's often a major headache. Unless you
buy something worth several hundred dollars, your
refund won't be worth the delays, incidental expenses,

and headaches that complicate the lives of TISVATR (Tourists in Search of VAT Refunds).

Even in jolly old England you should use traveler's checks and a money belt. Theft is a part of tourism and the careless are sitting ducks. A money belt (see catalog) is peace of mind. You can carry lots of cash safely in a money belt.

If you'll be traveling exclusively in Great Britain, buy traveler's checks in pounds sterling. If you get Barclays checks (you'll find a Barclays Bank in nearly every English town), you might sometimes avoid the commission banks charge for changing money. I bring a credit card only because it's necessary to rent a car. Spend cash, not plastic, as you travel. Save time and money by changing plenty of money at a time. (Many banks charge £2 per exchange.)

Americans have an easy time in Britain with weights and measures. The British use Fahrenheit, miles, inches, pounds, and ounces.

Travel Smart

This itinerary assumes you are a well-organized traveler who lays departure groundwork on arrival in a town, reads a day ahead in this book, uses the local tourist information offices, and enjoys the hospitality of the British people. Ask questions. Most locals are eager to point you in their idea of the right direction. Use the telephone, wear a money belt, pack along a small pocket notebook to organize your thoughts, and practice the virtue of simplicity. If you insist on being confused, your trip will be a mess. Those who expect to travel smart, do.

Scheduling

Your overall itinerary is a fun challenge. Read through this book and note special days such as festivals, colorful market days, and closed days for sights. Sundays have pros and cons as they do for travelers in the U.S.A. (special events, limited hours, shops and banks closed, limited

public transportation, no rush hours). Saturdays are virtually weekdays. Popular places are even more popular on
weekends—especially sunny ones, which are sufficient
cause for an impromptu holiday in the soggy British Isles.
It's good to alternate intense and relaxed periods. Every
trip (and every traveler) needs at least a few slack days. I
followed the biblical "one in seven" idea religiously on
my last trip.

To give you a little rootedness, I've minimized one-
night stands. Staying two nights in the same place, even
with hectic travel days before and after, makes for a less
grueling trip than changing accommodations daily. One-
night stands are less of a problem if you travel in the off-
season.

The daily suggested schedules and optional plans take
many factors into account. I don't explain most of those,
but I hope you take the schedules seriously. The day
plans, although realistic, are very fast, and those who
want to have more of a vacation than a busy-bee experience have my hearty blessing to slow down and see less
in a more relaxed way. I wish everyone had 30 days to do
this tour.

When to Go
July and August are peak season—my favorite time—with
the best weather and the busiest schedule of tourist fun.
But peak season is crowded and more expensive than
travel in other seasons. Most of us travel during this
period, and this book tackles peak season problems,
especially those of finding a room. "Shoulder season"
travel (May, early June, September, and early October) is
easier. Shoulder season travelers get minimal crowds,
decent weather, sights and tourist fun spots still open,
and the joy of being able to just grab a room almost
whenever and wherever they like. Winter travelers find
absolutely no crowds, but limited hours. The weather can
be cold and dreary, and nightfall will draw the shades on
your sightseeing well before dinner time.

In my experience, British weather is reliably unpredictable (but mostly bad), and July and August are not much better than shoulder months. May and June are often lovely. Conditions can change several times in a day, but rarely is the weather extreme. Daily averages throughout the year range between 42 degrees and 70 degrees, and temperatures below 32 degrees or over 80 degrees are cause for headlines.

Climate Chart: The chart below gives average day-time temperatures and average number of days with more than a trickle of rain.

	Jan	Feb	Mar	Apr	May	Jun	Jul	Aug	Sep	Oct	Nov	Dec
London	43	44	50	56	62	69	71	71	66	58	51	45
	15	13	11	12	11	11	12	11	13	14	15	15
S. Wales	45	45	50	56	61	68	69	69	65	58	51	46
	18	14	13	13	13	13	14	15	16	16	17	18
York	43	44	49	55	60	67	70	70	65	57	49	45
	17	15	13	13	13	14	15	14	14	15	17	17
Edinburgh	42	43	46	51	56	62	65	64	60	54	48	44
	17	15	15	14	14	15	17	16	16	17	17	18

Telephoning in Britain

Take advantage of the telephone. You can make long distance calls direct and easily, and there's no language barrier. I call ahead to arrange for rooms, check opening hours, reserve theater tickets, and even call home rather than mess with postcards.

The old pay phones take 10p coins. After you dial and someone answers, you hear the famous "rapid pips." Your voice can't be heard until you push in the coin. Talk until you hear more pips, which mean it's time to sign off or pop in 10p more. Newer phones ingeniously take any coin from 2p to £1, and a display shows how your money supply's doing. Only completely unused coins will be returned, so put in biggies with caution. The new and ever more prevalent telephone card system is wonderfully convenient. Buy £2, £4, or £10 cards at newsstands, hotels, tourist offices, or post offices and use them for ease and economy.

Area codes for calling long distance are a major pitfall.

England has about as many area codes as we have
prefixes. For local calls, just dial the three- to seven-digit
number. Area codes for "trunk" calls are listed by city on
phone booth walls, through directory assistance, and
throughout this book. Area codes in Britain and Europe
begin with 0. For a telephone directory, see the
Appendix.

   If dialing from another country, you replace that 0 with
the country code. For instance, England's country code is ·
44, inner London's code is 071. My London B&B's number is 727-7725. To call it from the U.S.A., I dial 011 (international code), 44 (British code), 71 (London's area code
without the 0), 727-7725. To call it from York, I dial 071
(London) 727-7725. To call the U.S.A. direct from England,
I dial 010 (international code), 1 (U.S.A. code), 206 (my
Seattle area code), and the seven-digit number. International calls are easiest on the new phones that take phone
cards or bigger coins. Note: London's old area code (01)
has been replaced by 071 for inner London (nearly everything we'll hit) and 081 for outer London. These days,
calling from home is easiest and cheapest with a credit
card. Access numbers are: AT&T—0800-8900-11;
MCI—0800-89-02-22.

Recommended Guidebooks

This small book is your blueprint for an inexpensive,
hassle-free trip. Although it's enough information, I'd
supplement it with a fatter, fine-print, directory-type
guidebook and some good maps. I know it hurts to
spend $30 or $40 on extra books and maps, but when
you consider the improvements they'll make in your
$2,000 vacation—not to mention the money they'll save
you—not buying them would be perfectly penny wise
and £ foolish. Here's my recommended list of supplemen-
tal information.

   Get a general, low-budget, directory-type guidebook
listing a broader range of accommodations, restaurants,
and sights. Which one you choose depends on your
budget and style of travel. My favorite by far is *Let's Go:*

Great Britain and Ireland, written and thoroughly updated annually by Harvard students (new editions come out each January). *Let's Go* covers big cities, villages, countryside, art, entertainment, budget room and board, and transportation. It's written for students on student budgets, and even though I'm not one, I use it every year. For cultural and sightseeing guidebooks, *The American Express Pocket Guide to England and Wales* and the AmExCo guide to London by Mitchell Beazley are compact and packed with handy information, including a rundown on local art, history, and culture, a list of all major sights, maps, and a helpful listing of hotels and restaurants for those with a little more money. The tall, green Michelin guide to London is also good. *Kidding Around London* (Santa Fe, N.M.: John Muir Publications, 1990) is a new guidebook that makes London fun and meaningful for traveling kids.

Europe Through the Back Door, my book, gives you the basic skills, the foundations that make this demanding 22-day plan possible. It has chapters on minimizing jet lag, packing light, driving vs. train travel, finding budget beds without reservations, changing money, theft and the tourist, travel photography, long distance telephoning in Europe, ugly-Americanism, traveler's toilet trauma, laundry, and itinerary strategies and techniques. The book also includes special articles on 40 exciting nooks and undiscovered crannies that I call "Back Doors." Six of these are in the British Isles.

Mona Winks, by Rick Steves and Gene Openshaw (Santa Fe, N.M.: John Muir Publications, 1989; see back-of-book catalog), takes you through Europe's 20 most frightening and exhausting museums with fun, easy-to-follow, two-hour self-guided tours. In London, *Mona* leads the way through the British Museum, the National Gallery, and the Tate Gallery.

Books and Maps to Buy in England: Most English bookstores, especially in tourist areas, have good selections of maps. I found a road atlas very useful for my basic overall needs (three miles to one inch, covering all of Britain, put out by the Ordnance Survey or by Bartholomew, available in tourist information offices, gas stations, or bookstores for about £7). For this itinerary, I'd also pick up much more detailed maps for the Cotswold region, North Wales, Windermere Lake District, West Scotland, and North York Moors.

Foyles' Bookstore in London (near Tottenham Court Road tube stop) has the best selection of guides and maps anywhere in Britain. WH Smith stores, the "English B. Dalton's" found in nearly every city, carry a good selection of guidebooks, maps, and local information. *2 to 22 Days in Great Britain* is published in England under the name *Great Britain in Your Pocket*. As you travel, you'll find racks of tempting little books at virtually every stop. The traditional finale of all British tourist attractions is ye olde gift and book shoppe.

Each town's energetic tourist office provides lots of good printed material. Take advantage of this wealth of fascinating and helpful information. For a complete list of all you'll need that can be picked up in one stop at London's National Tourist Information Centre (see shopping list in Day 1).

Tourist Information Centres (TIs)
Virtually every British town has a helpful tourist information center eager to make sure your visit is as smooth and enjoyable as possible. Take full advantage of this service. Arrive (or telephone) before they close with a list of questions and a proposed sightseeing plan for them to confirm and most likely improve upon. They can help you find a room and give you maps, eating advice, and walking tour guides. Whatever your question, they've got the answer.

Before your trip send a postcard requesting general information and any specific information you might need (such as a list of upcoming festivals) to the British Tourist Authority: 40 W. 57th St., New York, NY 10019, tel. 212/581-4700, or 350 S. Figueroa, Rm. 450, Los Angeles, CA 90071, tel. 213/628-3525.

Flying to London

Flying to London is your major expense, and a little study can save you a bundle. Fares and regulations to England vary all over the U.S.A. From the East Coast, you can fly cheapest by studying the *New York Times* travel section, comparing standby and cut-rate prices with the best deal your travel agent can give you. From the West Coast, you can't beat what a good travel agent will sell you. You need an agent who knows and enjoys budget European travel. Read the newspapers, talk to other travelers, but most of all establish a loyal relationship with a good agent. London is about the cheapest European destination from the States, and if you can avoid summer travel it's even cheaper.

By Car or Train?

It's a big question—and there is a correct answer. Cars and trains have pros and cons. Cars are best for three or more traveling together and people packing heavy gear, scouring the countryside, and doing peak-season room-finding with no reservations. Train and bus are best for single travelers, city-to-city travelers, and blitz tourists.

My choice for this itinerary is footloose and fancy-free by rental car. Britain's train system is speedy and extensive but uses London as a hub, so "across-the-grain" travel can be tedious. Still, you can modify this 22-day plan, as explained in the Appendix, supplement where necessary by bus, and have a fine 22-day BritRail tour.

Car Rental

If you plan to drive, rent a car through your travel agent well before departure. Car rental for this tour is cheaper if arranged in the U.S.A. than if arranged in Britain. You'll want a weekly rate with unlimited mileage. Plan to pick up the car at Heathrow Airport on Day 4 and drop it off 19 days later at Cambridge. If you drop it off early or keep it longer, you'll be credited or charged at a fair, prorated price. Keep in mind that you may drop off the car at any location if you have a change of plans. Budget, Hertz,

Avis, Kenning, and Godfrey Davis all allow Heathrow
pickups and Cambridge drop-offs. See which is cheapest
through your agent. Small local rental companies (such as
Terminal Car Rental and Alamo Car Rental) can be sub-
stantially cheaper but not as flexible.

I normally rent the smallest, least expensive model
(such as a Ford Fiesta). For a bigger, roomier, and more
powerful inexpensive car, move up to the Ford 1.3-liter
Escort category (about £30 per week more).

For peace of mind, I splurge for the CDW insurance
(collision damage waiver, about £6 per day), which gives
a zero-deductible rather than the standard value-of-the-
car "deductible." Remember, minibuses are a great budget
way to go for five to nine people.

Driving British
Driving in Britain is basically wonderful—once you
remember to stay on the left and after you've mastered
the "roundabouts." Please be warned: every year, I get a
few cards from traveling readers advising me that for
them, driving British was very difficult and dangerous.
Here are a few random tips.

Your U.S.A. license is all you need. A British Automobile Association membership comes with most rentals.
Be sure you know how it works. Gas (petrol) costs more
than $3 per gallon and is self-serve. Know what octane
(star) rating your car takes, push the correct button, and
pump away. Seat belts are required by law in the front
seat. Speed limits are 30 mph in town, 70 mph on the
motorways, and 60 mph elsewhere. (Time estimates in
this book assume a law-abiding speed.) Avoid big cities
whenever possible. Most have modern ring roads to skirt
the congestion. Rush hours are basically the same as ours.
The shortest distance between any two points is usually
the motorway.

Parking is confusing. One yellow line means no parking Monday through Saturday during work hours. Double yellow lines mean no parking at any time. Broken yel-

low means short stops are okay, but always look for explicit signs or ask a passing passerby.

Even in small towns, parking in Britain can be a royal headache. Rather than fight it, I just pull into the most central and handy car park I can find; follow the big blue "P" signs. I keep a bag of 10p coins in the ashtray for parking meters. Copy your car key as soon as possible so you won't get locked out and so your partner enjoys access to the car. Buy some Windex to clean your windows with each morning.

Sleeping in Britain

Thank God Britain has such lousy hotels, because the bed and breakfast alternative is second to none, with a homey charm that I prefer to even the most luxurious hotels. Generally, the less atmosphere a hotel has, the more it charges. Guest houses and bed and breakfasts (B&Bs) seem to be popping up all over the place to fill that void.

On this trip, I'm assuming you have a reasonable but limited budget. Skip hotels. Go the B&B way. Where there's a demand, there will be a supply. B&Bs hang out their shingles where you need them, and any town with tourists has a TI that can book one for you or give you a list and point you in the right direction. In the absence of a TI, ask people on the street for help. B&Bs are family-run, usually just a large home with a few extra rooms to let. They charge £12 to £18, or $22 to $36 (more in London), and always include the "full English breakfast." How much coziness and extra tea and biscuits is tossed in varies tremendously.

The B&Bs I've recommended are nearly all stocking-feet comfortable and very "homely," as they say in England. My prerequisites for recommending a place are that it must be: friendly; in a central, safe, quiet neighborhood; clean, with good beds, a sink in the room and shower down the hall; not in other guidebooks (therefore it is filled mostly by English travelers); and willing to hold a room until 4:00 p.m. or so without a deposit. (In certain cases, my recommendations don't meet all these prerequisites.)

I promised the owners of the places I list that you would be reliable when you make a telephone reservation; please don't let them (or me) down. If you'll be delayed or won't make it, call in. They can normally fill your bed only with the help of the local tourist office room-finding service, which usually closes at 5:00 or 6:00 p.m. Americans are notorious for "standing up" B&Bs. Being late is no problem if you are in telephone contact.

A few tips: B&B proprietors are selective as to whom they invite in for the night. Risky-looking people find many places suddenly full. If you'll be staying for more than one night you are a "desirable." Sometimes staying several nights earns you a better price—ask about it. The TI generally takes about a 10 percent commission for those it sends. If you book direct, the B&B gets it all. Nearly all B&Bs have plenty of stairs. Expect good exercise and be happy you packed light. If one B&B is full, ask for guidance. (Mention this book.) Owners usually work together and can call up an ally to land you a bed. Unless I'm relying on a particular recommendation, I enjoy shopping for my B&B, touring three places and choosing the best. "Twin" means two single beds, and "double" means one double bed. If you'll take either one, let them know or you might be needlessly turned away.

B&Bs are not hotels. If you want to ruin your relationship with your hostess, treat her like a hotel staff person. Americans are notorious for assuming they'll get new towels each day. The British don't, and neither will you. Hang them to dry and reuse.

B&Bs normally advertise with prominent signs in their yard or windows. The British Tourist Authority's "Stay on a Farm" booklet is a great listing of farmhouse B&Bs.

The British Tourist Board is now rating hotels and B&Bs with a uniform crown system. B&Bs are rated as follows: no crowns (basic, clean, one bath per 12 people, safe); one crown (no nylon bed linen, washbasin in the

room, one bath per eight people); two crowns (tea and coffee in room on request, TV in room or lounge, luggage
help); three crowns (one-third of rooms with bathroom);
four crowns (three-fourths of rooms with bathroom,
nearly a hotel); five crowns (all with private bath and
W.C., valet, porters, virtually a high-class hotel). Some
idealistic guest house proprietors are refusing to bow to
the pressure to fill their B&Bs with all the gimmicks and
extras. They continue to offer just a good bed, traditional
breakfast, and a warm welcome. They go unlisted but are
an excellent value. In the First World, simplicity is sub-
versive.

Room-finding is very easy from September 15 through
June 1. At other times of year, call ahead, try to arrive
early, and take advantage of room-finding services in
most TIs. They charge about £1 to make reservations in
another city but can save you lots of headaches. You can
do this tour any time of year without advance reservations for lodgings, but if you don't need flexibility or
want a particular place, call ahead. The local policy: for
reservations of more than a week in advance, they'll ask
for a signed traveler's check to be sent; less than a week,
and they'll hold a room until about 5:00 p.m.

Youth Hostels: Britain has 400 youth hostels of all
shapes and sizes. They can be historic castles or depressing huts, serene and comfy or overrun by noisy children,
but they're never expensive.

Hostels charge about £4 to £10 a night (depending on
grade of hostel and age of hosteler) and normally provide
hot meals at budget prices and a member's kitchen for
even cheaper eating. Most are wonderfully located and
pleasantly run, but hostels are not B&Bs. You need a
membership card (available in the U.S.A. or Britain), and
there's a dorm for men and one for women. They lock up
through midday and usually at 11:00 p.m. Big city hostels
are normally more institutional and less comfortable than
town and country ones. Off-season hosteling is easy and
so uncrowded that married couples can often share a
room. In peak season, most hostels fill up by dinner time.

There is absolutely no age limit to hosteling. In fact, youth hostelers over the age of 55 get half-price membership cards. Many English hostelers have been at it for 50 years. Use the small but very helpful British hostel guidebook, available at any hostel. If you're traveling alone, this is the best way to defeat hotel loneliness. Hostels are also a tremendous source of local and budget travel information. If you hostel selectively, you'll enjoy historical and very interesting buildings.

Eating in Britain

I think English food is just fine. But then, when I was in college I liked dorm food. True, England isn't famous for its cuisine and probably never will be, but we tourists have to eat. If there's any good place to cut corners to stretch your budget in Britain, it's in eating. Here are a few tips on budget eating in Britain.

The English (or Scottish or Welsh) "fry" is famous as a hearty way to start the day. Also known as a "heart attack on a plate," the breakfast is especially feasty if you've just come from the land of the skimpy continental breakfast across the Channel. Your standard "fry" starts healthy enough with juice and cereal (or porridge). Top-notch places give both and occasionally even grapefruit sections. (Try Weetabix, a soggy English cousin of shredded wheat. Scotland serves great porridge.) Next, with tea or coffee, you get a heated plate with a fried egg, very lean Canadian-style bacon, a pretty bad sausage, a grilled tomato, and often a slice of delightfully greasy pan toast, baked beans, and sautéed mushrooms. The last course is a rack of toast with butter and marmalade. (The purpose of the rack is to allow the toast to cool quickly and crisply.) This meal tides many travelers over until dinner.

One problem with B&Bs and this itinerary is that many don't serve breakfast until 8:30 or 9:00 a.m. If you need an early start, ask politely if it's possible. Consider skipping breakfast on occasion if a quick start is important.

For lunch on this tour, I'd picnic. Restaurants cost too much time and money. Outfit your car with a back-seat

cardboard pantry. My standard shopping list includes:
boxes of orange juice (Del Monte is best), fresh bread,
tasty English cheese, meat, a tube of Colman's English
mustard, local eatin' apples, bananas, small tomatoes,
chocolate-covered "Digestive Biscuits," rice crackers,
gorp or nuts, paper towels, disposable cups, and any local
specialties I bump into. English open-air markets and
supermarkets are fine. I often eat "meals on wheels" en
route to save 30 precious minutes and enjoy a relaxed-
pace meal while driving. A small plastic water bottle, zip-
lock baggies, and a Swiss army knife are handy.

Although British restaurants are fairly expensive, there
are plenty of cheap alternatives: fish-and-chips joints,
Chinese and Indian take-outs, cafeterias, B&Bs that serve
evening meals, and your typical, good ol' greasy spoon
places. Throughout Britain I've had very good luck following recommendations from my B&Bs. Bakeries have
meat pies, microwaves, pastries, and cartons of milk—
ideal for fresh, fast, cheap lunches.

Pubs are a basic part of the British social scene and,
whether you're a teetotaler or a beer-guzzler, they should
be a part of your travel here. Pub is short for "public
house." It's an extended living room where, if you don't
mind the stickiness, you can feel the pulse of Britain.
Most traditional atmospheric pubs are in the countryside
and in smaller towns. Unfortunately, many city pubs have
been afflicted with an excess of brass, ferns, and video
games. In any case, smart travelers use the pubs to eat,
drink, or get out of the rain and make new friends.

Pub grub is getting better each year. Pubs offer far and
away the best eating values in Ireland and Britain. You'll
get a basic budget hot lunch or dinner in friendly surroundings. It's so cheap mainly because you order it
yourself at the bar. Many pubs have an attached restaurant
and vice versa. Eat the same food for much less money at
the pub. *The Good Pub Guide*, published annually by the
British Consumers Union, is excellent.

Pubs generally serve assorted meat pies (such as steak
and kidney pie, shepherd's pie), curried dishes, fish,

quiche and vegetables, and invariably chips and peas.
Servings are hearty, service is quick, and dinners cost
from $5 to $10. Your beer or cider adds another dollar or
two. Free water is always available. A "ploughman's
lunch" is a modern traditional English meal that nearly
every tourist tries. . .once. Eat only at pubs that advertise
their food and have crowds eating there. Some pubs serve
only lousy microwaved snacks.

The British take great pride in their beer. They think
that drinking beer cold and carbonated, as Americans do,
ruins the taste. To the average American, a good English
beer tastes flat, smooth and room-temperature. Experi-
ment with the English "bitters," ales, and local brews.
Stick to whatever's on tap and try the draft cider. . .cau-
tiously. When you want just a good, cold, unexotic beer
like you get at home, ask for a lager. Pub hours vary. The
strictly limited wartime hours were finally ended, and
now pubs can serve beer from 11:00 a.m. to 11:00 p.m.
Drinks are served by the pint or the half-pint. (It's not
considered macho for a man to order just a half; I order
mine with quiche.) Teetotalers can order a soft drink or a
"shandy." People go to a "public house" to be social.
They want to talk. Pubs are the next best thing to relatives
in every town.

Who's legal in pubs? In England, by law, children under
14 are not allowed to enter; youths from 15 to 17 are
allowed in but won't be served beer. Anyone 18 or over
can be served alcohol. This is not consistently enforced.

Ugly Americanism
We travel all the way to Great Britain to experience something different—to become temporary locals. Americans
have a knack for finding certain truths to be God-given
and self-evident—things such as cold beer, a bottomless
coffee cup, long, hot showers, and driving on the right-
hand side of the road. One of the beauties of travel is the
opportunity to see that there are logical, civil, and even
better alternatives. If there is a British image of you and

me, we are big, loud, rich, aggressive, and a bit naive. (The American worker earns twice what his British counterpart does, and taxes, unemployment, and the cost of living are all higher for the British worker.)

Still, I find warmth and friendliness throughout Great Britain. An eagerness to go local and an ability—when something's not to my liking—to change my liking ensure that I enjoy a full dose of British hospitality. Try it, it works!

Europeans, in general (after you weed out the inordinately noisy elements), admire and support a strong America. The British like us even though many will remind us that our high-flying national eagle is not perfectly house trained. While Europeans look bemusedly at some of our Yankee excesses—and worriedly at others—they nearly always afford us individual travelers all the warmth we deserve.

Freedom

This book's goal is to free you, not chain you. Please defend your spontaneity as you would your mother. Use this book to sort Britain's galaxy of sights into the most interesting, representative, diverse, and efficient 22 days of travel. Use it to avoid time and money-wasting mistakes, to get more intimate with Britain by traveling without a tour—as a temporary local person. This book is a point of departure from which to shape your best possible travel experience. Only a real dullard would do this entire tour exactly as I've laid it out. Personalize! Anyone who has read this far has what it takes intellectually to do this tour on his or her own. Be confident and militantly positive; relish the challenge and rewards of your own planning.

Send Me a Postcard, Drop Me a Line

Although I do what I can to keep this book accurate and up to date, things are always changing. If you enjoy a successful trip with the help of this book and would like to

share your discoveries, please send your tips, recommendations, criticisms, witticisms, or corrections to Rick
Steves, 109 4th Avenue North, Box C-2009, Edmonds,
WA 98020. All correspondents will receive a year's subscription to our Back Door Travel quarterly newsletter
(it's free anyway).

Thanks, and Bon Voyage!

AS TAUGHT IN *EUROPE THROUGH THE BACK DOOR*

Travel is intensified living—maximum thrills per minute and one of the last great legal sources of adventure. In many ways, the less you spend, the more you get.

Experiencing the real thing requires candid informality— going "Through the Back Door."

Affording travel is a matter of priorities. Many people who "can't afford a trip" could sell their cars and travel for two years.

You can travel anywhere in the world for $40 a day plus transportation costs. Money has little to do with enjoying your trip. In fact, spending more money builds a thicker wall between you and what you came to see.

A tight budget forces you to travel "close to the ground," meeting and communicating with the people, not relying on service with a purchased smile. Never sacrifice sleep, nutrition, safety, or cleanliness in the name of budget. Simply enjoy the local-style alternatives to expensive hotels and restaurants.

Extroverts have more fun. If your trip is low on magic moments, kick yourself and start making things happen. If you don't enjoy a place, it's often because you don't know enough about it. Seek the truth. Recognize tourist traps. A culture is legitimized by its existence. Give a people the benefit of your open mind. Think of things as different but not better or worse.

Of course, travel, like the world, is a series of hills and valleys. Be fanatically positive and militantly optimistic. Travel is addicting. It can make you a happier American as well as a citizen of the world. Our Earth is home to five billion equally important people. It's wonderfully humbling to travel and find that people don't envy Americans. They like us, but with all due respect, they wouldn't trade places.

Globe-trotting destroys ethnocentricity and encourages the understanding and appreciation of various cultures. Travel changes people. Many travelers toss aside their "hometown blinders," assimilating the best points of different cultures into their own character.

The world is a cultural garden. We're tossing the ultimate salad. Raise your travel dreams to their upright and locked position and join us.

DAY 1   Arrive in London, visit the tourist information office to lay the groundwork for the next three weeks, get set up in your B&B, and take an evening orientation walk through the heart of London.

DAY 2   Take the two-hour introductory double-decker bus tour of London before the 11:30 changing of the guard at Buckingham Palace. Then walk through the Piccadilly area to colorful Covent Gardens for lunch. Spend the afternoon touring the Tower of London with a Beefeater guide and dodge drools at the crown jewels. Then take the Thames cruise from the bloody tower to Westminster, landing at the foot of Big Ben. Check out Westminster Abbey, possibly visit the Halls of Parliament to see the House of Commons in action, grab some pub grub for dinner (with coffee for jet-laggards), and finish the day enjoying one of London's plays.

DAY 3   London has much more to see. Spend the morning touring the British Museum. Climb to the summit of St. Paul's, pop in to view the action at "Old Bailey," peep at the high criminal court, complete with powdered wigs and robes, or tour the London Stock Exchange before finishing your sightseeing day in the smashing Museum of London.

DAY 4   Pick up your rental car at Heathrow Airport to avoid crazy London driving and drop by Salisbury to see its cathedral. Wander through the mysterious Stonehenge and Avebury stone circles before joyriding through several thatch-happy villages and into Bath.

DAY 5   Tour Bath's Roman and medieval mineral baths before taking a coffee break in the elegant Pump Room. Follow a local guide for a two-hour walking tour through the fascinating highlights of England's trend-setting Old

Tour Route: 22 Days in Great Britain

HIGHLANDS
LOCH NESS
INVERNESS
SCOTLAND
-16-
+ BEN NEVIS
PITLOCHRY
OBAN -15-
○ EDINBURGH
-17,18-
GLASGOW
HADRIAN'S WALL
N. IRE.
-19- ○ DURHAM
BELFAST
LAKE DIST. -13,14-
NORTH YORK MOORS
-20-
YORK ○ -21-
BLACKPOOL -12-
DUBLIN
LIVERPOOL
ENGLAND
IRELAND
-11- ○ RUTHIN
CAERNARFON
IRONBRIDGE GORGE
SNOWDONIA
○ -10-
COVENTRY -9-
WARWICK STRATFORD
ROSSLARE
WALES
COTSWOLD
CAMBRIDGE -22-
TINTERN -7-
STOW -8-
CARDIFF
BATH -5-
WELLS
-4-
LONDON -1,2,3-
-6-
GLASTONBURY
SALISBURY
STONEHENGE

0   40   80
MILES

○ OVERNIGHTS
• DAY VISITS

DCH

World Hollywood. Spend the afternoon browsing and touring England's greatest collection of costumes—300 years of fashion history, from Anne Boleyn to Twiggy.

DAY 6   Today, side trip south, exploring the haunted and entertaining Wookey Hole Caves, Wells with its medieval center and striking cathedral, and mystical Glastonbury, home of Avalon, King Arthur, and the Holy Grail. Evening free in Bath.

DAY 7   Drive into Wales, through its capital of Cardiff, and to the Welsh Folk Museum, a park full of restored old houses, offering an intimate look at this fascinating culture. After a scenic drive up the Wye River Valley, past Tintern Abbey, and through the Forest of Dean, set up at Stow-on-the-Wold in the heart of the Cotswold Hills.

DAY 8   Spend half the day in the Cotswold Hills, savoring the most delicious of England's villages, the quintessence of quaint. Then visit Blenheim Palace.

DAY 9   After a morning in Shakespeare's hometown, Stratford, tour England's finest medieval castle at Warwick and see the inspirational Coventry Cathedral—a charred ruin from the "blitz" with a shiny new church built more with love than with nails.

DAY 10   Today is devoted to the birthplace of the Industrial Revolution. In the Ironbridge Gorge on the Severn River, you'll find a series of museums that take the visitor back into those heady days when Britain was racing into the modern age and pulling the rest of the West with her. Then it's into the romantic beauty of North Wales, setting up in Ruthin.

DAY 11   Circling scenic and historic North Wales, tour a woolen mill, the Caenarfon Castle, awesome Mount Snowdon, and a bleak slate mine, arriving home in time to indulge in a medieval Welsh banquet complete with harp, singing wenches, mead, daggers, and bibs.

DAY 12   From Edenism to Hedonism, drive from idyllic North Wales to Blackpool, England's Coney Island. Britain's most popular tourist attraction—which nearly all Americans skip—is six miles of fortune-tellers, fish-and-chips, amusement piers, beaches, warped mirrors, and hordes of Englanders. It's recess!

DAY 13   For another splash of contrast, drive into the pristine Lake District, where Wordsworth's poems still shiver in trees and ripple on ponds. After a short cruise and a six-mile walk around the loveliest of these lovely lakes, check into a remote farmhouse B&B.

DAY 14   A pilgrimage to Wordsworth's famous Dove Cottage is in order before you enjoy this free day to relax, recharge, and take the hike you like, maybe even write a poem.

DAY 15   Now you'll steam north into Scotland, past bustling Glasgow, along the scenic Loch Lomond for a six-hour drive to the Highlands. Blaring bagpipes and swirling kilts accompany dinner tonight.

DAY 16   Today's all-day joyride features the stark beauty of Glencoe, scene of a bloody clan massacre, a drive from coast to coast along the Caledonian Canal, and Loch Ness. Even if you don't see the monster, you will tour a grand castle and enjoy some fine Highland scenery. After a visit to Culloden, the site of the last battle on British soil and the end of Bonnie Prince Charlie and Scottish hopes, you'll zip down from Inverness to Edinburgh.

DAY 17   Edinburgh! one of Europe's most entertaining cities. After a tourist office orientation, you'll cover the Royal Mile, touring the Edinburgh Castle, the Holyrood Palace—where the queen stays when she's in town—and everything in between. This is the colorful city of Robert Louis Stevenson, Walter Scott, and Robert Burns.

DAY 18   There's much more to see and do in Edinburgh: take in a concert in the park, the elegantly Georgian new town, the best shopping in Scotland, and an
evening of folk music and dance.

DAY 19   Two hours south of Edinburgh, Hadrian's Wall
reminds us that Britain was an important Roman colony
2,000 years ago. After a walk along the ramparts and
through a fine Roman museum, it's on to the fascinating
Beamish Open-Air Museum for a look at Yorkshire life in
the dawn of our century. Finally, you'll tour the Durham
Cathedral, England's finest Norman church.

DAY 20   After a morning in the lonesome North York
Moors with their time-passed villages, bored sheep, and
powerful landscapes, set up in the city of York in time to
enjoy an introductory walking tour led by an old Yorker.

DAY 21   York has more than its share of blockbuster
sights. Divide this day between the great York Minster,
the Jorvik exhibit (the best Viking museum anywhere),
and several engrossing hours in the York Castle
Museum—a walk with Charles Dickens.

DAY 22   After a three-hour drive to Cambridge, check
your bags at the station, turn your car in, and spend the
afternoon exploring England's loveliest cluster of colleges. Cambridge, with its sleepy river, lush green
grounds, mellow study halls, helpful tourist office, and
old streets clogged with bicycles, is worth all the time
you can muster today before catching the hour-long train
ride into London.

   The circle is complete, and you've experienced the
best 22 days Britain has to offer. Blimey, next year you
might want 22 more.

FLY TO LONDON

On this busy first day, you'll fly halfway round the world, then set up and settle in for a night in one of Europe's most exciting cities—London.

Suggested Schedule

Depart U.S.A.

Arrive at airport in London, travel downtown. Follow "Arrival in London" instructions carefully.

Check into your hotel, hostel, or B&B.

Visit the TI at Victoria Station (possibly en route to your hotel) for London and Britain information and play tickets.

Make trip-organizing phone calls from your hotel.

Ride the bus downtown to Westminster Bridge for your first night walk.

(Note: If your plane arrives in the morning, you might have time to take the Round London orientation this afternoon, freeing up some time tomorrow.)

Flying Away

Call the airport before leaving home to be sure your plane's on schedule. Combat boredom and frustration from the inevitable delays and lines by bringing something to do—a book, journal, darts, or some handwork. If you haven't already read this book carefully from cover to cover, do so, making notes during the flight. Expect delays and remember that no matter how long it takes, flying to England is a very easy, space-age way to get there. If you land safely on the day you hope to, it's been a smashing success.

   To minimize jet lag (body clock adjustment, stress):

   ■ Leave well rested. Schedule a false departure day one day early. Plan accordingly and, even at the cost of hecticity the day before, enjoy a peaceful last day.

   ■ During the flight, minimize stress by eating lightly,

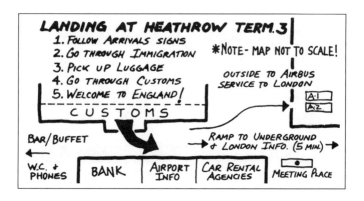

avoiding alcohol, caffeine, and sugar. Drink juice. ("Two glasses of orange juice, no ice please.")

■ Sleep through the in-flight movie—or at least close your eyes and fake it (unless you're reading *2 to 22 Days in Great Britain*).

■ Change your watch (and your mind) to London time. Upon arrival, get exercise, daylight, and fresh air.

Arrival in London

When you fly to Europe, you lose a day. If you leave on Friday, you land on Saturday. From the airplane, follow the "arrivals" signs to baggage and customs. Heathrow Airport has a reputation for being confusing. Ask questions. Collect your baggage and proceed to customs. The customs official will take a quick look at your passport, ask you a few questions to be sure you're adequately financed and not a spy, marvel at how light you're packing, and wave you through.

After customs, you'll pop into throngs of waiting loved ones. You'll see a bank (open 24 hours daily) and an information desk. Change some money and buy a £5 bag of 10p coins for phone calls and future parking. At the airport terminal information desk, pick up a London map, ask about transportation downtown by Airbus or subway (tube), and get directions to the Heathrow TI. You might also drop by your car rental agency's desk to confirm

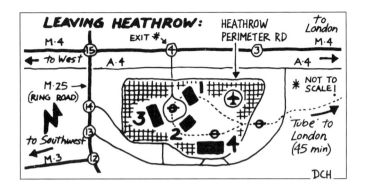

your pick-up plans on Day 4. Then follow the signs to the subway or "underground" (a long walk on a moving ramp) to the TI. This TI (open 9:00 a.m. to 6:00 p.m. daily) is much less crowded than the Victoria Station TI downtown. Get whatever information you'd like and consider buying your telephone card, Heritage Pass (discount ticket to many of Britain's top sights), and your subway pass (Travel Card, £ 2.30 per day). Then you can hop on the subway or walk back into the airport to catch the Airbus.

Anyone flying British Air will land in the new and impressive Terminal 4, where you'll find a bank with lousy rates and Airbus and tube service to downtown.

Transportation to Downtown
The fastest and easiest cheap way into London is by tube (£2.50) or Airbus (£5), depending on where your hotel is. Buses leave Heathrow constantly: A1 goes to Victoria Station, and A2 goes to Euston Station with stops along the way. Most of my hotel recommendations are on the A2 Airbus line near Notting Hill Gate (one stop past the Hilton Hotel).

Although the tube works fine, I prefer taking the Airbus into London—no connections underground and a lovely view from the top of the double-decker. Ask the driver to remind you when to get off.

Most flights arrive at Heathrow, but some charters go

into Gatwick Airport, halfway between London and the south coast. No problem. Trains shuttle between Gatwick and Victoria Station four times an hour (a 30-minute, £7 ride).

Orientation

London, more than 600 square miles of urban jungle with seven million struggling people, many of whom speak English, is a world in itself, a barrage on all the senses. On my first visit, I felt very, very small. It's much more than museums and famous landmarks. It's a living, breathing organism that somehow manages to thrive.

London Town has changed dramatically in recent years, and many visitors are surprised to find how "un-English" it is. Whites are actually a minority now in major parts of a city that once symbolized white imperialism. Arabs have pretty much bought out the area north of Hyde Park. Fish-and-chips shops are now outnumbered by Chinese take-outs (or "fee 'n' chee shops" as some locals call them). Most hotels are run or at least staffed by people with mysterious foreign accents, while outlying suburbs are huge communities of West Indians, Indians, and Pakistanis. London is learning—sometimes fitfully— to live as a microcosm of its formerly vast empire.

With just three nights and two days here, you'll get no more than a quick splash in this teeming human tide pool. But hopefully, with a quick orientation, you'll get a good sampling of its top sights, history, cultural entertainment, and ever-changing human face.

London has all the pitfalls of any big city, but if you're on the ball, informed, and well-organized, it won't cost a fortune, you won't get ripped off, and you'll leave ready for the more peaceful countryside but looking forward to your return.

Transportation in London

London's taxis, buses, and subway system make a private car unnecessary. In a city this size, you must get comfortable with its public transportation. Don't be timid; take the bull by the tail, and in no time you'll have London by the horns. (Or I suppose you could do it the other way around.)

Taxis: Big, black, carefully regulated cabs are everywhere. I never met a crabby cabbie in London. They love to talk and know every nook and cranny in town. Rides start at £1 and stay reasonable. There are often extra charges (legitimate ones) added on, but for a short ride, three people in a cab travel at tube prices. If the top light is on, just wave one down. If that is difficult, ask for directions to a nearby taxi stand. Telephoning is unnecessary; taxis are everywhere.

Buses: London's extensive bus system is easy to follow if you have a map listing the routes (as most tourist maps do). Signs at the stops list exactly where the buses go. Conductors are terse but helpful. Ask to be reminded when it's your stop. Just hop on, take a seat, and relax. (Go upstairs for the best view.) You'll be ticketed whenever the conductor gets around to it. Buses and taxis are miserable during rush hours, 8:00 to 10:00 a.m. and 4:00 to 7:00 p.m. Rides range in price from 70p to more than £1.

Subway: The London "tube" is one of this planet's great people movers. Every city map includes a tube map. Rip one out and keep it in your shirt pocket. You'll need it. Navigate by color-coded lines and north (always up on the map), south, east, or west. Buy your ticket at the window or from coin-op machines to avoid the line before descending to the platform level. Then hang onto it, giving it to a checker as you leave the system. Read system notices and signs carefully; they explain the tube's latest flood, construction, or other problem. Ask questions of locals and watch your wallet. You'll find that "tubing" is by far the fastest long-distance transport in town. It used to be fiercely expensive but now costs a reasonable 60p to £2.50 per ride. Remember, "subway" means pedestrian underpass in "English." For tube and bus information, call 222-1234.

London Tube and Bus Passes: Nearly every tourist should take advantage of one of the inexpensive three-,

four-, and seven-day Travel Cards. Available on the spot
in tube stations, they give you unlimited transportation
on all buses and subways. When buying individual tube
tickets, keep in mind that children under age 5 travel free
and ages 5 through 14 get 60 percent off. Anything within
the Circle Line is within one zone and costs 60p. Cheap
day returns for long trips are discounted 33 percent. Consider the one-day passes for the Central Zone (travel to
any destination on or within the Circle Line, except before
9:30 a.m. on weekdays; cost: £2.50), which includes
nearly all major places of touristic interest.

London Information

You can't McGoo London. Get information and use it.
Good guidebooks abound. The free London transport
and tourist map (available at the TI, some tube stations,
and hotels) is good enough, but the first-class map (50p)
is ideal.
  London Tourist Information Centres are located at
Heathrow Airport, in Victoria Station (tel. 730-3488,
open daily 9:00 a.m. to 8:30 p.m., stops answering the
phone at 5:30 p.m., shorter hours in winter), at Selfridges
on Oxford Street, and at Harrods (regular store hours).
The crowded Victoria Station office has a great selection
of books covering all of Britain, a room-finding service
(not cheap), and a helpful staff with a huge arsenal of
fliers, lists, maps, and printed advice. They can also sell
you theater tickets.
  For the best listing of what's happening that week
(plays, movies, restaurants, concerts, exhibitions, walking
tours, protests, what to do with children, and so on), pick
up a current copy of *What's On* at any newsstand. (*Time
Out* and *City Limits* are hip and more opinionated ver-
sions of *What's On*. You can also telephone 222-8070 for
a taped rundown on "Children's London.")
  Bring your schedule and a checklist of questions to the
handiest London Tourist Office. Go over your London
plans, buy a ticket to a play, and pick up these publications:

Walking tour brochure, theater guide
Directory of TIs around Britain
What's On (or *Time Out* or *City Limits*)
Quick Guide to London
London map

National Tourist Information

The energetic British Tourist Authority has opened an impressive new National Tourist Information Centre just off Piccadilly Circus (12 Regent St., tel. 730-3400, open Monday through Friday 9:00 a.m. to 6:30 p.m., Saturday and Sunday 10:00 a.m. to 4:00 p.m.). In this huge center, you'll find an extensive travel bookshop, an expensive (£5 charge) room-finding service for the entire British Isles (including London), a British Rail information desk, and an American Express Bank, as well as a helpful tourist information desk. This is the place to gather whatever information, maps, and advice you'll need for your entire trip. So that you can pull into each stop on this 22-day plan with a tour map and well prepared, I recommend a map for each city you'll visit as well as the following:

■ *A Britain Road Atlas* (the AA edition), £5
■ *Let's Go: Britain* (if you don't already have it), £10
■ *Youth Hostel Association 1991 Guide* (if you plan to hostel), £1.95
■ American Express Guides to *London* and *England*, £4.95.
■ The *Penguin London Mapguide*, £1.95
■ *Stonehenge and Avebury* (picture book), £1.50
■ *Wales Tourist Map*, £1.35
■ *Tourist Guide to North Wales* £1.25
■ *Tourist Guide to South Wales*, £1.25
■ *Cotswolds Wyedean Official Tourist Map* (covering Tintern to Coventry), £2.25
■ *Stay On A Farm*, a booklet listing farmhouse B&Bs
■ *Lake District Tourist Map* (Ordinance Survey), £2.40
■ *The Good Guide to the Lakes* (Hunter Davies), £2.95

■ *The Michelin Green Guide to Scotland*
■ *Leisure Map Touring Scotland*, £1.95
■ *The Good Pub Guide* (current year, £10, published by Britain's Consumers' Association), an excellent reference listing more than 5,000 pubs. Especially good if you plan to eat in pubs. I referred to it almost daily.

All that buying is going to lighten your money belt by a few pounds, but two people spending two bucks a day for this information can be set up to really travel smart. You are your own guide. Be a good one.

Within a block of the National Tourist Information Centre, you'll find the Scottish Tourist Centre (19 Cockspur St., tel. 930-8661) and the Welsh Tourist Centre (34 Piccadilly, tel. 409-0969).

Accommodations in London's Nottinghill Gate Area

Inexpensive, central, and comfortable—pick two. With London's great tube system, I'll sacrifice centrality for a cheery place that won't ruin my budget. London has hundreds of hotels but few great deals. There's no need, however, to spend a fortune or stay in a dangerous, depressing dump. Plan on spending about £45 (about $90) for a basic, decent double with breakfast.

Reserve your London room in advance with a phone call direct from the States (dial 011/44/71/London phone number). Assure the manager that you'll arrive before 4:00 p.m., leave your credit card number, or send a signed $100 traveler's check. (Leave the "pay to" line blank and include a note explaining that you'll be happy to pay cash upon arrival so they can avoid bank charges if they'll just hold your check until you get there.)

My favorite home base for London is the Nottinghill Gate area. It's residential, with quick and easy bus or tube access to downtown, on the A2 Airbus line from Heathrow (2nd stop), relatively safe (except for the dangerous, riot-plagued Nottinghill Carnival, the last weekend of August), and, for London, very "homely."

Here are a few of my favorite hotels. All are near the

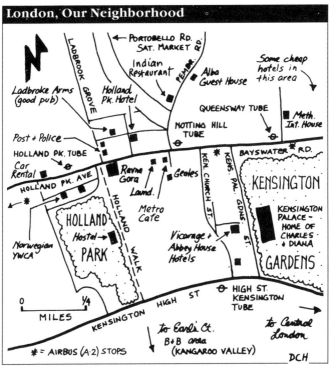

London, Our Neighborhood

Holland Park or Nottinghill Gate tube station. Reminder: throughout this book, the following words are used only to indicate these price ranges in room-and-board listings: Beds (per person with breakfast): cheap = under £13, inexpensive = £13-17, moderate = £17-23, and expensive = more than £23. Three-course meals without drinks: cheap = under £4, inexpensive = £4-6, moderate = £6-10, expensive = more than £10.) A pound (£) is worth roughly $2.

Vicarage Private Hotel is very popular, family-run, and elegantly British in a quiet, classy neighborhood midway between the Nottinghill Gate and High Street Kensington tube stations near Kensington Palace (moderate-expensive, 10 Vicarage Gate, Kensington, London W8 4AG, tel. 071/229-4030). Make reservations long in advance with a phone call followed by one-night deposit.

Abbey House Hotel (expensive, 11 Vicarage Gate, Kensington, London, W8, tel. 727-2594) is similar in almost every way to its neighbor, the Vicarage Private Hotel. It's a few pounds more expensive and a bit less cozy. A one-night deposit is required.

Hotel Ravna Gora—Located just across from the Holland Park tube station. Formerly Mr. Holland's mansion, now it's a large B&B run by supporters of the long-exiled king of Serbia. Eccentric and well worn; still, you won't find a more comfortable or handy place for the price. Manda and Rijko take good care of their guests while downstairs the Serbian royalists quaff beer and dream of a glorious restoration. Royal TV room, good English breakfast (moderate-expensive, 29 Holland Park Ave., London WII, tel. 727-7725).

Alba Guest House (moderate-expensive, 53 Pembridge Villas, London, W11, tel. 727-8910) is very small, friendly, and family run in a funky but pleasant locale at the foot of colorful Portobello Road, a block from the Nottinghill tube stop. It's run by Raymond Khoo. They don't take reservations; call on arrival in London.

Dean Court Hotel—This place is wild and crazy, with good basic facilities, and full of Aussies (inexpensive in shared rooms, 57 Inverness Terrace, tel. 229-2961).

Holland Park Hotel—The most "hotelesque" (and expensive) of any of these places. Even so, Richard Taylor runs this good value with a personal touch. TVs in each room; continental breakfast in your room (as in most London hotels these days), quiet, pleasant street, will accept telephone credit card reservations (expensive, 6 Ladbrook Terrace, W11 3PG, tel. 071/792-0216).

Inverness Court Hotel—This elegant, well-worn, turn-of-the-century hotel has comfortable, spacious public rooms, hotelly bedrooms, a handy, safe location, and a staff that barely speaks English (very expensive, #1 Inverness Terrace, W2 3JL, tel. 229-1444).

Methodist International House—This is a Christian residence filled mostly with Asian and African students, great if you want a truly worldwide dorm experience.

Weekly rates, laundry facilities. (Cheap in shared doubles or triples with dinner, 2 Inverness Terrace, W2 3HY, near Bayswater tube, tel. 229-5101.)

Norwegian YWCA (Norsk K.F.U.K.)—For women under 26 only (and men with Norwegian passports), this is an incredible value—lovely atmosphere, on quiet stately street, piano lounge, TV room, study, all rooms with private shower, all three meals included. They have mostly quads, so those willing to share with strangers are most likely to get a place (cheap, 52 Holland Park, W11 3R5, tel. 727-9897). It's tight in July and August. They'll hold a room for a phone call. (I wonder what's easier—a sex change or getting a Norwegian passport?)

Accommodations in Other Areas (tel. area code: 071)
Catholic International Chaplaincy—Another gem, open to both men and women, provides a TV lounge, study room, self-serve kitchen, breakfast, and a very pleasant atmosphere (moderate, 34 Adolphus Road, London N4 2AY, tube: Manor House, tel. 802-9673).

Coleman Lodge Hotel—Big, hip, scruffy but comfortable, this is the best cheap hotel I've found in the center. Student oriented, with a bar and a TV lounge (inexpensive doubles, 31 Craven Hill Gardens, W2, near Lancaster Gate and Bayswater tube stations, tel. 723-5988).

Queensway Hotel (expensive, 147 Sussex Gardens, London W2, tel. 723-7749) is one block from Paddington in a good area.

Mary Ward's Guest House—Worth the travel time, this great and friendly value is in Clapham Common (cheap, 98 Hambalt Rd., Clapham Common, London, tel. 673-1077), 20 minutes by tube or bus 88 and a 10-minute walk.

Harlingford Hotel (moderate-expensive, 61 Cartwright Gardens, tel. 387-1551) is very well run and comfortable. Located near the British Museum (tube: Russell Square) on a crescent with several other good budget B&Bs.

Lynwood Guest House—Out of London (25 minutes by train) near Gatwick Airport (15 minutes by train), this place offers a cozy, friendly alternative to big city lodging. Easy parking, near the train station, genuinely caring and gracious (moderate, 50 London Rd., Redhill, Surrey RH1 1LN, tel. 0737/766894).

Basic Downtown B&B Areas: Near Victoria Station, Belgrave Road, Warwick Way, and St. George Way are lined with reasonable, nondescript B&Bs. Nearby Ebury Street has some of the best values.

Hostels—£8-10 beds: Holland Park King George VI Memorial Hostel (cheap, Holland Walk, Kensington, London W87QU, tel. 937-0748) is a formal, institutional IYHF hostel in a lovely park with 10- to 20-bed rooms, good dining hall with cheap meals, and self-serve facilities. It is well run and usually full. Arrive early. **Holland Park Independent Hostel** (cheap, 31 Holland Park Gardens, W14, tel. 602-3369) is scruffy, well run, 68 beds (mostly 4- to 8-bed coed dorm with a few twins), members' kitchen, takes reservations. Its sister hostel (41 Holland Park, tel. 229-4238) is bigger, scruffier, hipper, and a lovely alternative to the bushes. **Palace Court Hotel** (cheap, 12-14 Pembridge Square, Bayswater W2, tel. 727-4412) is the winner for backpackers who hate IYHF curfews and formality. A very creatively run place with small dorms and a few twins on a pleasant square next to the royal kids' Montessori school. Bar, beer, video games, laundry, cheap meals, lots of friends, more Aussies than Americans.

London's cheapest and generally grottiest beds: **Tent City** (£4, tel. 743-5708, open June through September, tube: East Acton) and **Tonbridge Club** (£2, tel. 837-4406, all year, students only, tube: Kings Cross).

Food

London has plenty of fine restaurants—at very high prices. If you want to dine (as opposed to eat), check out the extensive listings in *What's On*. The thought of a £20 meal generally ruins my appetite, so my London dining is limited mostly to unremarkable but inexpensive alternatives.

Restaurants near Recommended Nottinghill Gate B&Bs: on Hillgate Street (near the Coronet Theatre) is **Costas** at #18 for good fish and Greek food and the **Hillgate Pub** with good food and famous hot saltbeef sandwiches. The **Modhubon** Indian restaurant at #29 Pembridge Road (tel. 727-3399) is worth the moderate splurge, as is the **Arc** on Kensington Palace Gardens Street. The **Churchill Arms** pub is a hot local hangout with a great Thai restaurant attached (Kensington Church St.,). For my favorite pub grub in the area, eat at the **Ladbroke Arms** (see map).

Fish-and-chips joints are still popular and easy to find. The best "chippie" in town in a comfy setting near my recommended B&Bs is the very popular **Geale's** (with a hard "G," inexpensive, 2 Farmer Street, just off Nottinghill Gate behind the Gate Theatre, open Tuesday through Saturday 12:00 noon to 3:00 p.m. and 6:00 p.m. to 11:00 p.m., tel. 727-7969). Get there early for a place to sit and the best fish.

Maggie Jones (expensive, 6 Old Court Pl. off Kensington Church St., W8, near the High Street Kensington tube stop, tel. 937-6462) is very English and serves my favorite £15 London dinner. If you eat well once in London, eat here. **The Twin Brothers Restaurant** (expensive, 51 Kensington Church St., W8, tel. 937-4152) is small, serving cozy, candlelit dinners, near the recommended Vicarage Hotel.

Pub grub is your most atmospheric budget option. Many of London's 7,000 pubs (I counted them myself one night) serve fresh, tasty buffets under ancient timbers with hearty lunches and dinners priced around £4. Ethnic restaurants from all over the world more than make up for the basically lackluster English cuisine. Eating Indian or Chinese is "going local" in London. It's also going cheap.

Eating in church, heavenly light meals on a monk's budget: **St.-Martin-in-the-Fields Restaurant** (inexpensive, 839-4342, underneath the church by the same name on Trafalgar Square, tel. 839-4342, daily 10:00 a.m. to 9:00 p.m., Sunday 12:00 noon to 8:00 p.m.) is a fine buffet in a crypt with great atmosphere. **Wren at St. James Church coffeehouse** (two minutes off Piccadilly, at 35 Jermyn St. open 12-6) is in a pleasant garden next to one of Wren's best churches. St. John's Church (Smith Sq. near Westminster Abbey) has the **Footstool** restaurant in its brick-vaulted crypt.

Stockpot (cheap, 40 Panton St. off Haymarket near Piccadilly, daily 8:00 a.m. to 11:30 p.m.) is famous and rightly popular for its budget but tasty meals.

Oodles (inexpensive, 128 Edgware Road near Marble Arch, tube: Edgeware) serves oodles of traditional food at good prices.

The Carvery (expensive, Regent Palace Hotel on Glasshouse St., just 20 feet off Piccadilly Square, Monday through Saturday 12:00 noon to 2:30 p.m., 5:15 p.m. to 9:00 p.m., Sunday 12:30 p.m. to 2:30 p.m. and 6:00 p.m. to 9:00 p.m.) serves an all-you-can-eat buffet of beef, Yorkshire pudding, dessert and coffee included—a carnivore's delight. Carvers help you slice.

Slenders Whole Food Restaurant and Juice Bar (inexpensive, Paternoster Sq., 41 Cathedral Place near St. Paul's tube station, Monday through Friday 9:30 a.m. to 6:15 p.m.) serves fast, healthy, tasty vegetarian meals. And, between Slenders and St. Paul's is the **Sir Christopher Wren Pub**, serving excellent, inexpensive lunches in fun surroundings. (Eat in the pub, not the restaurant.)

Eating near Covent Gardens: This colorful, boutiquish center of cozy modern London street bustle is filled with antique shops, doily cafes, interesting bookshops, street entertainers, and people. It's a great place to find an inexpensive lunch. Try the small delis around Neal's Yard (end of Monmouth St.), **Porter's** (17 Henrietta Sq., fun, Old World, more expensive), **Diana's Diner** (39 Endall St., hearty, traditional), or the many pubs offering meals. For the best buys, you're wise to walk a block or two away from the eye of this touristic tornado. It's hard to go wrong in a little tea and sandwich deli.

Of course, the picnic is the fastest and cheapest way to go. There are plenty of good grocery stores, fine park benches, and polite pigeons in Britain's most expensive city.

If nothing here sounds tasty, **London's Restaurant Switchboard** (tel. 444-0044, Monday through Saturday until 8:00 p.m.) can give you lots of thoughts for food.

First-Night Walk

Now that you're set up for the night, it's time to enjoy a very relaxed introduction to London. This walk is a pleasant orientation and also a great fresh-air-and-exercise way to stay awake on the jet-lag evening of your arrival.

Catch a bus down to Westminster Bridge (12 from Nottinghill Gate; sit on the top deck. Relax until you get to your stop, the first stop after the bridge.) Walk downstream to Jubilee Promenade for a capital view then, for that "Wow, I'm really in London!" feeling, cross the bridge to view the floodlit Houses of Parliament and Big Ben up close. Grandma Lee's Restaurant, across from Big Ben next to the tube station, serves good, light meals (view upstairs).

For a special thrill back home, call home from a pay phone near Big Ben (there's one on Great George Street, across from Parliament Square) at about three minutes before the hour. As Big Ben chimes, stick the receiver outside the booth and prove you're in London (dong dong dong dong . . . . dong dong ding dong).

Then cross Whitehall, noticing the Churchill Statue in the park. (He's electrified to avoid the pigeon problem that stains so many other great statues.) Walk up toward Trafalgar Square. Stop at the barricaded and guarded little Downing Street to see #10, home of the British prime minister. Break the bobbie's boredom—ask him a question. Just before Trafalgar Square, drop into the Clarence Pub for a reasonable dinner or pint of whatever you fancy. From Trafalgar, walk to thriving Leicester Square and continue to Piccadilly. St. Martin's crypt (on Trafalgar

Square, under St. Martin-in-the-Fields church) has a fine cafeteria and café.

For seediness, walk through Soho (north of Shaftes-bury Avenue) up to Oxford Street. From Piccadilly or Oxford Circus you can taxi, bus, or subway home. Why not teach yourself the subway system now? With all this activity, you're more likely to sleep well on the tradition-ally fitful first night in Europe.

DAYS 2 AND 3
THE BEST OF LONDON

The sights of London alone could easily fill a 22-day trip. Today and tomorrow will be spent enjoying as many of these sights as time, energy, and sanity will allow. Obviously, this is only a suggested itinerary. You'll have two days, Briggs, in which to pick and choose among all the things listed here.

Suggested Schedule Day 2

8:00	Breakfast, tube or bus to Marble Arch.
9:00	Catch Round London Tour.
11:00	Taxi to Buckingham Palace for 11:30 changing of the guard. Or stroll, window-shop, and people-watch your way from Marble Arch to Covent Garden (or see Speaker's Corner if it's Sunday).
1:00	Lunch in Covent Garden.
2:00	Walk the Strand to the Temple tube station and subway to Tower Hill. Tour the Tower of London, starting with the Beefeater Tour.
5:00	Sail from the Tower to Westminster Bridge, enjoying a 30-minute commentary on the Thames. The Westminster Abbey is open until 6:00 p.m. and the Visitors Gallery in the Houses of Parliament is open, when in session, until 10:00 p.m.
7:00	Pub dinner near your theater.
8:00	Most plays start at 8:00; enjoy the one of your choice.

Sightseeing Highlights

After considering nearly all of London's tourist sights, I have painfully pruned them down to just the most important (or fun) for a first visit. You won't be able to see all of these, so don't try. You'll keep coming back to London. After 15 visits myself, I still enjoy a healthy list of excuses to return.

Suggested Schedule Day 3

8:00	Breakfast, easy morning, any last tour planning.
10:00	British Museum.
1:00	Lunch near St. Paul's in the Christopher Wren pub or, for a light, healthier meal, try Slender's Wholefood Restaurant at 41 Cathedral Place.
2:00	Explore St. Paul's: climb to the top for the view. Many other Wren churches are nearby, as well as Old Bailey and the ornate medieval guild hall.
4:00	Walk to the Museum of London for the best possible London history lesson.
Evening	A performance in the impressive Barbican Center.

▲**London Transit System Red Bus Tour**—This orientation tour is a good introduction. The city bus company gives these 90-minute "stay on the bus and enjoy a light once-over of all the most famous sights with a great commentary" doubledecker tours for £8, £7 if you prepurchase at information centers. Tours leave daily on the half hour from 9:00 a.m. to 4:00 p.m. plus 6:00 p.m. from Marble Arch, Piccadilly Circus, and Victoria Station (Victoria Street). No reservations necessary (tel. 222-1234).

▲**Walking Tours**—Every day, several walking tours explore specific slices of London's past. These are listed in *What's On* and the TI has plenty of fliers. You just show up at the announced location, pay £3, and enjoy two hours of Dickens, the Plague, Shakespeare, Jack the Ripper, or whatever is on the menu. Evenings feature organized pub crawls and "ghost walks."

▲▲▲**Tower of London**—You'll find more bloody history per square inch here than anywhere in Britain. Don't miss the entertaining Beefeater tour (free, leaving regularly from inside the gate) of this historic fortress, palace, prison, and host to more than three million visitors a year. Britain's best armory and most lovely Norman chapel are in the White Tower. The crown jewels are the best on earth—and consequently have long lines for viewing midday in July and August. To avoid the crowds, arrive at 9:30 and go straight to the jewels, doing the Tower later. (Tower hours: Monday through Saturday 9:30 a.m. to 5:45 p.m., last entry 5:00 p.m., Sunday 2:00 p.m. to 5:45 p.m. The long, but fast-moving, line is worst on Sundays. £5.50 entrance, tube: Tower Hill.)

There is a great TI across from the Tower entrance (pick up their "Sightseeing Near the Tower" brochure). St. Katherine Yacht Harbor, chic and newly renovated, is just past the freshly painted (and now open, £2, tel. 930-4097) Tower Bridge, with mod shops. A classic old pub, the Dickens Inn, is fun for a drink or lunch. Boat tours with a very good commentary sail regularly between Westminster Bridge and the tower (30 minutes, £2). The best remaining bit of London's Roman Wall is just north of the tower (tube: Tower Hill).

▲▲▲**Westminster**—The Abbey, Houses of Parliament, and Whitehall. Westminster Abbey is a crowded collection of England's most famous tombs. It reminds me more of a refugee camp waiting outside St. Peter's gates than an English hall of fame. Historic, thought-provoking but a bit overrated (open daily 9:00 a.m. to 6:00 p.m., until 8:00 p.m. on Wednesday, £2, £4 with "super tour").

The Houses of Parliament are too tempting to terrorists to be open to tourists, but you can view the House of Commons when it's sitting. (If Big Ben is floodlit, the House is in session.) Monday through Thursday 4:15 p.m. to 10:00 p.m.—long waits until 6:00 p.m.; use St. Stephens entrance. No bags allowed. Notice the magnificent hammer-beamed Westminster Hall on the left as you go through security. Information tel. 219-4272. Don't miss the view from the bridge. You won't actually see Big Ben, the 13-ton bell inside the neo-Gothic tower; you'll hear him, though. Remember, these old-looking buildings are neo-Gothic—just nineteenth century, reflecting the Victorian move away from neoclassicism and into a more Christian, medieval style. Best view is from across Westminster Bridge.

The Underground

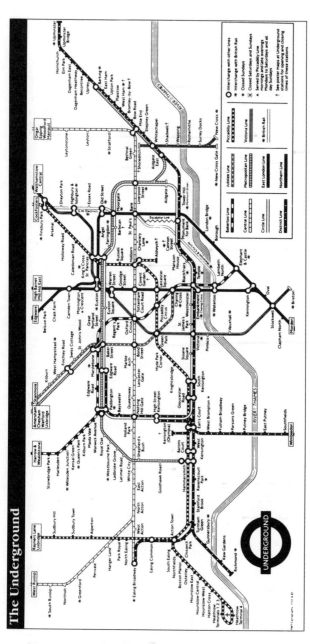

Copyright London Transport Executive

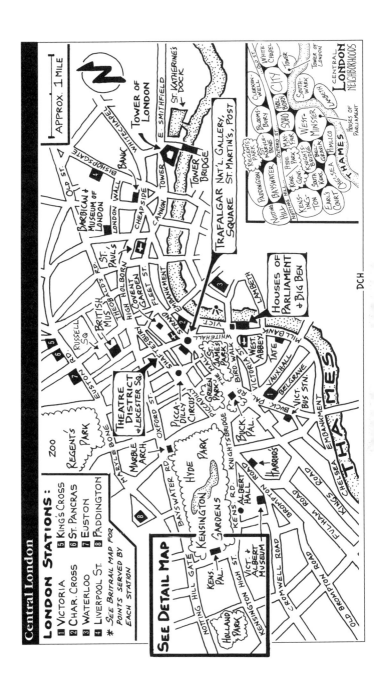

Central London

LONDON STATIONS:

1. VICTORIA
2. CHAR. CROSS
3. WATERLOO
4. LIVERPOOL ST.
5. KING'S CROSS
6. ST. PANCRAS
7. EUSTON
8. PADDINGTON

* SEE BRITRAIL MAP FOR POINTS SERVED BY EACH STATION

APPROX. 1 MILE

N

SEE DETAIL MAP

ZOO

REGENT'S PARK

MARYLEBONE

MARBLE ARCH

OXFORD ST.

Theatre District + LEICESTER SQ.

RUSSELL SQ.

BRITISH MUS.

THEOBALD'S RD.

HIGH HOLBORN

ST. PAUL'S

BARBICAN + MUSEUM OF LONDON

OLD ST.

BISHOPSGATE

LONDON WALL

BANK

CHEAPSIDE

CANNON

TOWER

Tower of London

ST. KATHERINE'S DOCK

E. SMITHFIELD

TOWER BRIDGE

FLEET ST.

COVENT GARDEN

SHAFTESBURY

PICCADILLY

PICCADILLY CIRCUS

GREEN PARK

ST. JAMES'S PARK

THE MALL

BIRD WALK

WHITEHALL

STRAND

EMBANKMENT

VICT.

LAMBETH

Houses of Parliament + BIG BEN

WEST. ABBEY

TATE

MILLBANK

VAUXHALL

BELGRAVE

VICT. BUS STN.

VICTORIA

BUCK. PAL.

BUCKINGHAM PALACE RD.

KNIGHTSBRIDGE

HARRODS

BROMPTON RD.

KENS. RD.

ALBERT HALL

HYDE PARK

BAYSWATER RD.

KENSINGTON GARDENS

KENS. PAL.

NOTTING HILL GATE

KENSINGTON HIGH ST.

HOLLAND PARK

VICT. + ALBERT MUSEUM

CROMWELL ROAD

OLD BROMPTON ROAD

FULHAM ROAD

KING'S ROAD

CHELSEA EMBANKMENT

THAMES

TRAFALGAR NAT'L. GALLERY, ST. MARTIN'S, POST SQUARE

DCH

CENTRAL LONDON NEIGHBORHOODS

THAMES

Houses of Parliament

PADDINGTON

BAYSWATER

NOTTING HILL

KENSINGTON

EARL'S COURT

KENS-ING-TON

REGENT'S PARK

MARYLE BONE

HYDE PARK

KNIGHTS BRIDGE

S. KENS.

BELGRAVIA

CHELSEA

PIMLICO

MAYFAIR

OXFORD ST.

SOHO

BLOOMS-BURY

CLERKEN-WELL

WEST-MINSTER

LAMBETH

SOUTH-WARK

CITY

WHITE-CHAPEL

HOL-BORN

TOWER

Tower of London

Whitehall, the center-of-government boulevard, runs from Big Ben to Trafalgar past lots of important but boring buildings. Stop by the barricade at 10 Downing Street (the British "White House"), the Horse Guards (10:00 a.m. to 4:00 p.m., 11:00 a.m. inspection, 4:00 p.m. colorful dismounting ceremony, the rest of the day—very still, lots of photos), the Banqueting Hall (England's first Renaissance building by Inigo Jones in 1625), and the atmospheric Clarence Pub.

▲▲**Cabinet War Rooms**—This is a fascinating walk through the underground headquarters of the British government's fight against the Nazis in the darkest days of the Battle for Britain. Churchill's room, the map room, and so on, are still just as they were in 1945 (open 10:00 a.m. to 6:00 p.m., closed Monday, £3.50, tube: Westminster; at Clive Steps on King Charles St. just off Whitehall). For more WW I and WW II memories, see the free and fascinating Imperial War Museum, located where the original Bethlehem Hospital for the Insane ("bedlam" for short) used to stand (daily 10:00 a.m. to 6:00 p.m., tube: Lambeth North).

▲▲**Trafalgar Square**—London's central square is a thrilling place to just hang out. There's Lord Nelson's towering column surrounded by giant lions (parts of the memorial are made from the melted-down cannon of his victims at Trafalgar), hordes of people, and even more pigeons. (When bombed, resist the impulse to wipe immediately—it'll smear. Wait for it to dry and flake off gently.) The square is the climax of most marches and demonstrations.

▲**National Gallery**—This is Britain's top collection of European painting from 1300 to 1900: van Gogh, Turner, Rembrandt, Leonardo, Velázquez, Botticelli, and impressionists. Monday through Saturday 10:00 a.m. to 6:00 p.m., Sunday 2:00 p.m. to 6:00 p.m., free, on Trafalgar Square. Tube: Charing Cross or Leicester Square. The National Portrait Gallery is just around the corner (free and exciting as somebody else's yearbook, tel. 839-3321).

▲▲**Piccadilly**—London's "Town Square" is surrounded

by fascinating streets and neighborhoods. Shaftesbury Avenue and Leicester Square teem with fun-seekers, theaters, Chinese restaurants, and street singers. Soho, to the north, seethes with sleazier activities and is worth at least a gawk. Walk up Berwick Street to Oxford Street and check out the formerly trendy, now tacky, Carnaby Street. The shiny new Trocadero Center (between Coventry and Shaftesbury just off Piccadilly) has the Guinness World Records Exhibit and the touristy but fun *London Experience* movie (10:20 a.m. to 10:20 p.m. daily, £ 2.75). The whole area between Regent Street, Oxford Street, Kingsway, and the Strand is titillating. Covent Garden is especially fun with its buskers, antique shops, liberal bookstores, far-out crowds, and imaginative eateries.

▲**Buckingham Palace and Changing of the Guard**—Overrated but almost required. You'll only see the back side of the palace, as the front faces a huge and very private park. The royal residence of London is never open to the public. (If the flag is flying, the queen is home.) The changing of the guard, almost daily in summer at 11:30 a.m., every other day in winter, is a mob scene. The best view is from the top of the Victoria Memorial (unless the bobbies are bouncing). The pageantry and parading are colorful and even stirring, but the actual changing of the guard is a nonevent. It's interesting mostly as an opportunity to see nearly every tourist in London gathered in one place at the same time. Hop in a big black taxi and say, "To Buckingham Palace, please." Stroll through nearby St. James Park.

▲**Hyde Park**—London's "Central Park" has more than 600 acres of lush greenery, a huge man-made lake, a royal palace (Kensington, worth touring), and the ornate neo-Gothic Albert Memorial across from the Royal Albert Hall. On Sunday early afternoons, check out Speaker's Corner (tube to Marble Arch). This is soapbox oratory at its best, the grass roots of democracy. I dare you to raise your voice and gather a crowd—it's very easy to do.

▲**Harrods**—This is one of the few stores in the world that combines size and class. Wonderful displays, elegant high teas, fingernail-ripping riots during the July sales. Harrods has everything from elephants to toothbrushes. Need some peanut butter?

Street Markets—If you like garage sales and people-watching, hit a London street market. The tourist office has a complete up-to-date list. A few of the best are: **Berwick Street** (tube: Piccadilly, Monday through Saturday, produce), **Jubilee Market** (tube: Covent Garden, 9:00 a.m. to 4:00 p.m., antiques and bric-a-brac on Monday, general miscellaneous Tuesday through Friday, crafts on Saturday and Sunday), **Kensington Market** (tube: High Street Kensington, Monday through Saturday 10:00 a.m. to 6:00 p.m., a collection of shops with modern and far-out clothing), **Petticoat Lane** (Middlesex St., tube: Liverpool St., Sunday 9:00 a.m. to 1:30 p.m., the largest, specializing in general junk), **Portobello Road** (near recommended B&Bs, tube: Nottinghill Gate; Monday through Friday general, Saturday flea market, 7:00 a.m. to 5:00 p.m.), and **Camden Lock** (a big flea market on Saturday and Sunday 9:00 a.m. to 6:00 p.m., tube: Camden Town). For a classier bit of window-shopping, cruise King's Road in Chelsea. Warning: street markets attract two kinds of people—tourists and pickpockets.

▲**Sir John Soane's Museum**—Every architect's favorite sight, this fascinating museum was the personally designed home of a wildly imaginative architect (near tube station Holborn, 13 Lincoln's Inn Field, Tuesday through Saturday 10:00 a.m. to 5:00 p.m., free).

▲▲▲**British Museum**—The greatest chronicle of our civilization anywhere, this immense museum can only be dipped into. Take a long walk—like hiking through Encyclopedia Britannica National Park. Then cover just two or three sections of your choice more thoroughly. The Egyptian, Mesopotamian, Greek (Parthenon), and Manuscripts (Magna Carta, Bibles, Beethoven, and the Beatles) sections are a few of my favorites. Free, open Monday through Saturday 10:00 a.m. to 5:00 p.m., Sunday 2:30 p.m. to 6:00 p.m., least crowded weekday mornings (tube: Tottenham Court Road).

▲▲**Tate Gallery**—One of Europe's great houses of art, the Tate specializes in British painting (fourteenth century through contemporary, especially Turner and Blake) and international modern art (Matisse, van Gogh, Monet). Learn about the mystical watercolorist Blake and the romantic nature-worship art of Turner. Lots of tours, a great gift shop (The gallery is free, Monday through Saturday 10:00 a.m. to 6:00 p.m., Sunday 2:00 p.m. to 6:00 p.m., tube: Pimlico, tel. 821-1313).

▲**Victoria and Albert Museums**—A surprisingly interesting collection of costumes, armor, furniture, and decorative arts. (Monday through Thursday and Saturday 10:00 a.m. to 6:00 p.m., Sunday 2:30 p.m. to 6:00 p.m. Closed Friday, £ 2 donation requested, tube: So. Kensington.)

Famous Auction?—London's famous auctioneers welcome the curious public. For schedules, telephone Sotheby's (493-8080) or Christie's (839-9060).

▲▲**The City of London**—When Londoners say "the City," they mean the one-square-mile business, banking, and journalism center that 2,000 years ago was Roman Londinium. The outline of the Roman city walls can still be seen in the arc of roads from Blackfriars Bridge to the Tower Bridge. Within the City are 24 churches designed by Christopher Wren.

A place near and dear to the busy people in three-piece suits and "tightly wrapped" umbrellas who clog that city by day is the Stock Exchange (free tours Monday-Friday, 9:45 a.m.-3:30 p.m.). Also worth a look is the Central Criminal Courts, known as "Old Bailey." An hour in the visitors' gallery is always fascinating (at Old Bailey and Newgate St., Monday through Friday 10:15 a.m. to 1:00 p.m., 2:00 p.m. to 4:00 p.m., closed or quiet in August, tel. 248-3277).

▲▲**St. Paul's Cathedral**—Wren's most famous church is the great St. Paul's, with an elaborate interior capped by a 365-foot dome. St. Paul's is the symbol of British resistance, as Nazi bombs actually bounced off it in World War II. It was the wedding church of Prince Charles and Lady

Di. Climb the dome for a great city view and some fun in the whispering gallery; talk into the wall and your partner on the far side can hear you. (Tours 11:00 a.m., 11:30 a.m., 2:00 p.m., 2:30 p.m., open daily 7:30 a.m. to 6:00 p.m., crypt and tower only until 4:15 p.m. Allow an hour to go up and down the dome—it's good exercise. Tube: St. Paul's.)

▲**Museum of London**—Take a hike through London history—from pre-Roman times to the Blitz (free, Tuesday through Saturday 10:00 a.m. to 6:00 p.m., Sunday 2:00 p.m. to 6:00 p.m., tube: Barbican or St. Paul's).

Entertainment and Theater

You could spend a lifetime being entertained in London. It bubbles with top-notch shows seven nights a week, reaching a boil each summer. The key to maximizing your entertainment pleasure is to take advantage of the "Time Out" or *What's On* magazine, available at most newsstands. You'll choose from classical, jazz, rock, and far-out music, Gilbert and Sullivan, dance, comedy, spectator sports, film, and theater.

I focus on the theater. London's theater rivals Broadway's in quality and beats it in price. Choose from the Royal Shakespeare Company, top musicals, comedy, thrillers, sex farces, and more. Performances are nightly except Sunday, usually with one matinee a week. Matinees (listed in a box in *What's On*) are cheaper and rarely sold out.

Most theaters are in the Piccadilly-Trafalgar area and are marked on tourist maps. Box offices, hotels, and TIs have a very handy "Theatre Guide" brochure listing everything in town. The quickest and easiest way to get a ticket is through a ticket agency (at Victoria TI or scattered throughout the theater district), but it's cheaper to go direct. Call the theater; many will hold tickets for you to pick up an hour before showtime. If it's "sold out," there's usually a way to get a seat. Call and ask how. If all else fails and money is no object, you can be voluntarily victimized by a scalper.

To reserve tickets from home, read the theater listing in

your library's London newspaper. Telephone the theater
of your choice and charge the ticket to your credit card.
Pick it up an hour before curtain time. I usually buy the
second-cheapest tickets. Many theaters are so small that
there's hardly a bad seat. "Scooting up" later on is less
than a capital offense. The famous "half-price booth" in
Leicester (pronounced "Lester") Square sells cheap
tickets the day of the show.

If you'll ever enjoy Shakespeare, it'll be here. The Royal
Shakespeare Company splits its April-through-January
season between the Royal Shakespeare Theatre in Stratford (tel. 0789/295623; recorded information tel.
0789/69191) and the Barbican Centre (open until 11:00
p.m. daily; tel. information: 628-2295; credit card ticket
booking tel. 638-8891). Tickets range in price from £ 4.50
to £20. For a complete schedule, write to the Royal
Shakespeare Theatre, Stratford-upon-Avon, Warwick-
shire, CV37 6BB, or call 0789/205301.

The ultimate round of beer: the London tube's Circle
Line makes 21 stops during each orbit. There just hap-
pens to be a pub near the entry of each of these subway
stops. A popular game is to race around trying to drink a
pint (or a half-pint) from each of the 21 bars between the
"old" pub hours (5:30 p.m. to 11:00 p.m.). Twenty-one
pints is about 2 gallons of beer. Locals prefer starting at
the Farrington stop. A few of the pubs are tough to
find—just ask the newspaper stand man for directions.

Helpful Hints
Very few London sights are open on Sunday before 2:00
p.m. Some Sunday morning activities: church, the Tube
Tour (11:00 a.m., tel. 504-9159), Round London bus tour,
a Thames cruise, Cabinet War Rooms, or markets at Petticoat Lane, Earl's Court, or Camden Locks. Those with
kids in tow can call 222-8070 for helpful ideas.

Be on guard here more than anywhere in Britain for
pickpockets and theft. You can leave anything you won't
need in a well-labeled bag at your hotel because you'll be
returning in three weeks.

Streets are named in segments. The London postal

code can be used as a rough compass, with districts numbered SW1, W1, NW6, and so on. The number is a rough measure of the distance from the city center (Trafalgar).

London's American Express office (6 Haymarket, SW1, tel. 930-4411, tube: Piccadilly) is open six days a week for mail pickups, seven days a week for money exchange. Dial 999 (free) for emergency help in London.

Itinerary Options—Day Trips from London

London is surrounded by exciting, easy day-trip destinations. Several tour companies take London-based travelers out and back every day (call Evan Evans at 930-2377, National Express at 730-0202, or Tourist Information for ideas). The British rail system works with London as a hub and normally offers round-trip fares that cost just a little more than their already reasonable one-way fares. See BritRail's handy "Day Trips from London" booklet. For the serious day-tripper, *Daytrips in Britain by Rail, Bus or Car from London and Edinburgh* is a great guidebook, including 60 one-day adventures, by Earl Steinbicker (Hastings House, ISBN 0-80381-93019, 12.95).

London uses a different train station for each destination region. For schedule information call the appropriate station: Kings Cross (northeast England; Scotland), 278-2477; Paddington (west and southwest England, south Wales), 262-6767; most others, 928-5100.

Things to Do in London for Your 22-Day Plan

■Reserve and pay for your hotel for your late-night return in three weeks.

■Reserve tickets for any special performances that are sold out now but not in three weeks (a Prom Concert, July-September, in the Royal Albert Hall, tel. 589-8212, or a ticket to a top play).

■Book a seat at the Stratford Theater if the RSC is playing during your Stow-on-the-Wold stay (Day 7). Tel. 0789/295623.

■Plan ahead for Edinburgh Festival (August 11-31 in 1991). Call the festival office at 031/225 5756 to book a ticket by credit card from June on. And while you're at it, book your Edinburgh room. Specific reservations to make (especially in July and August) for your 22-day plan: (1) B&Bs in Bath, Stow, Ironbridge, and Ruthin. You might want to call any others deeper into the tour if you have a particular favorite or are ready to commit yourself to a date; (2) Ruthin Medieval Banquet—book ahead, either direct or through a Ruthin B&B; (3) write to the Tower of London (H M Governor, Tower of London, London EC3) three weeks in advance, with an envelope stamped and addressed to your London hotel, requesting an invitation to the moving "ceremony of the keys." Say which night or nights you can come.

SALISBURY, STONEHENGE, BATH

Pick up your car, leave the big city, and tour the lively
market town and cathedral of Salisbury. Explore two mysterious stone circle reminders of England's ancient past—
Stonehenge and Avebury—and finally get set up in the
pride of Georgian England, Bath.

Suggested Schedule

9:00	Pick up car, drive to Salisbury.
11:00	Salisbury town and cathedral. Picnic on cathe-dral grounds (or skip Salisbury to leave Lon-don later or arrive in Bath earlier).
1:30	Ponder Stonehenge.
2:00	Drive to Avebury.
3:00	Don't hurry Avebury.
4:00	Follow small, scenic roads into Bath.
5:00	Arrive, set up in Bath.

**Transportation: London to Salisbury (90 mi.) to
Stonehenge (8 mi.) to Bath (30 mi.)**
Picking Up Your Car: London is a terrible place to learn
to drive British-style. Survivors recommend picking up
your rental car out of the city at Heathrow Airport. The
subway or Airbus will take you there stresslessly, where
major, eager rental agencies are lined up, all trying harder.
If you decide to pick up your car in London, Kenning Car
Hire (84 Holland Park Ave., W11, next to the Holland Park
tube station, tel. 727-0123) and Le Car Hire (40 Kensington Rd., W11, tel. 727-4426) are in "Our London Neighborhood" (see map).

Your rental car orientation is always rushed, but be sure
to understand the basics: locate the car manual, know
how to change a tire and what kind of gas to use, understand their breakdown policy and how to use the
Automobile Association membership that comes with
most car rentals. Ask the attendant for an extra key, a list

of drop-off offices, any map he can give you, and directions to Salisbury or Stonehenge. Before you leave, drive around the airport parking lot and get to know your car for five or ten minutes. Work the keys, try everything. Note the British arrangement of switches and signals; find problems before they find you.

London—Salisbury—Stonehenge: London, like most big cities, has a ring road, the M25. Wherever you are (airport or downtown) get on M25 and follow the "west" signs until you get to M3, which zips you toward Salisbury. After Basingstoke, take the A30 exit and you're 30 miles from Salisbury. Market towns like Salisbury are parking nightmares. Follow signs to "city center" and then into a central car park. From Salisbury, go to Amesbury via A345 where signs will get you to Stonehenge, two miles west. Stonehenge has a free car park with public rest rooms.

Stonehenge—Avebury—Bath: Next, continue north from Amesbury on A345 to the thatched village of Upavon. "A" roads are always faster, but in this case I'd take the tiny scenic road through the villages of Hilcott, Alton Priors, and West Kennett to Avebury. You won't find a legal parking place in the village of Avebury, so use the lot with the blue "P" for tourists. From Avebury, follow A4 west to Calne, A3102 south to the lovely thatched village of Sandy Lane on A342. Take the tiny lane west out of Sandy Lane to the Tourist Board's prize-winning Tudor village of Lacock. From there, take the A4 for the most beautiful approach into Bath.

If you have a road atlas book, be sure to take advantage of its city maps. In the case of Bath, navigate by bridges and landmarks. As usual, parking downtown is hopeless. Parking near your B&B shouldn't be too bad.

Good Pub Stops: In Upavon, the **Antelope Inn** serves a very good ploughman's lunch or supper. A possible stop on your way into Bath.

For a pleasant village evening, drive 30 minutes from Bath to Lacock—a tourist trap by day but charming after dark. The **Carpenter's Arms** serves fine pub grub.

Sightseeing Highlights
▲▲**Salisbury Cathedral and Market**—The Salisbury
Cathedral, with the tallest spire in England, is a fine reason to stop here. Admire its exterior, the cloister, the
chapter house with an original Magna Carta and a ring of
sculpted Old Testament scenes. See how many you can
identify and then ask a guard for a sheet of "answers."

Spend some time wandering through the old center of
town, particularly fun on market day (Saturdays and Tues-
days). I do my market chores here, buying a "brollie"
(umbrella) for 3, a "jumper" (sweater) for the wet and
nippy weather, and a few cassettes for my car tape deck.

▲▲**Stonehenge**—This is England's most famous stone
circle, built 4,000 years ago in the days of Egypt's
pyramids. These huge stones were brought all the way
from Wales to form a remarkably accurate celestial calen-
dar. Even today, every summer solstice (around June 21)
the sun sets in just the right slot, and Druids go wild. The
monument is roped off, so even if you pay the £2 entry
fee, you're kept at a distance. Although you can see it free
from the road, it's worth a closer look.

▲▲**Avebury**—The stone circle at Avebury is bigger, less
touristy, and I think more interesting than Stonehenge.
You're free to wander among 100 stones, ditches,
mounds, and curious patterns from the past, as well as
the village of Avebury, which grew up in the middle of
this 1,400-foot-wide Neolithic circle. Fascinating!

Take the one-mile walk around the circle. Visit the fine
little archaeology museum (not the local farm life one)
and pleasant cafe behind the village church. The Red
Lion Pub (tel. 06723/266) has good, inexpensive pub
grub. Notice the pyramid-shaped, ancient-manmade Sil-
bury Hill nearby.

Itinerary Options
Speed demons could check out Winchester, a pleasant
town with a great cathedral, en route to Salisbury (40
minutes extra road time). Also, if you're unable to spend a

day visiting Wells and Glastonbury later, and if you're thoroughly reserved for a room in Bath, you could skip Salisbury and Avebury and go from Stonehenge to Glastonbury (see the abbey, climb the tower) and on to Wells (park in the central square, see old town, bishop's palace, and great cathedral) before arriving late in Bath.

BATH, ENGLAND'S COVER GIRL

Bath is Europe's most underrated city. Any tour of Britain that skips Bath stinks. Two hundred years ago, this city of 80,000 was the Hollywood of Britain. If ever a city enjoyed looking in the mirror, Bath's the one. It has more "government listed" or protected historic buildings per capita than any other town in England. The entire city is built of creamy warm-tone limestone called "Bath stone." Bath beams in its cover-girl complexion. An architectural chorus line, it's the triumph of Georgian style. Bath's narcissism is justified.

Suggested Schedule

8:00	Breakfast.
9:00	Roman baths. Double check walking tour departure time posted outside. Rush the museum to catch the first (and least crowded) of the guided tours, which leave every 15 minutes starting at 9:15 from the actual bath (looks like a big swimming pool). You can go back into the museum after the tour.
10:00	Enjoy a coffee break; smack your lips to the tunes of a string trio in the elegant Pump Room above the museum (or take more time for the museum).
10:30	Take the city walking tour (depart in front of the Pump Room).
12:30	Your guide will probably end the tour at the Assembly Rooms. Browse downhill into the old shopping center to find lunch. The Royal Victoria Park nearby is ideal picnicking terrain.
3:00	Tour 1 Royal Crescent Museum.
4:00	Tour the Costume Museum in the Assembly Rooms. (Adjust your afternoon schedule to make the guided tour here. The last tour is normally at 4:30 p.m.)

Sightseeing Highlights

▲▲▲The Baths (Roman and Medieval)—For 2,000 years, high society has enjoyed the mineral springs at Bath. Londoners traveled to Aquae Sulis, as Romans called the city, so often to "take a bath" that finally the city became known as, simply, Bath. This town's hot, wet claim to fame is now a fine Roman museum with tours every 15 minutes. Only with the enthusiastic help of your guide will the complex of ancient Roman and medieval baths and buildings make sense. (Open 9:00 a.m. to 7:00 p.m. daily. Tours leave on the quarter hour throughout the day. £3.50.)

▲Pump Room—Just above the Roman baths, this elegant Georgian Hall is a visitor's best chance to be Old World elegant. Drop by to sip morning coffee (10:00 a.m. to 12:00 noon) to the rhythm of a string trio, or enjoy afternoon tea (3:00 p.m. to 5:30 p.m.) with piano entertainment. This is your opportunity to have a famous (but not especially good) "Bath bun" and drink the awfully curative water.

▲▲▲Walking Tours of Bath—These leave from in front of the Pump Room daily except Saturday at 10:30 a.m. (occasionally, at 2:30 p.m. and 7:00 p.m. from May through October). They are offered free by trained local volunteers who simply want to share their love of Bath with its many visitors. For a private (not free but reasonable) guide, call Gordon Tarrant at 0272/864463 or Patrick Driscoll at 0225/4629531. Otherwise, check with the TI on the same square.

▲▲▲Costume Museum—One of Europe's great museums, displaying 300 years of fashion one frilly decade at a time, is housed in Bath's elegant Assembly Rooms. Free tours leave mostly early or late in the day, and the guides are great. Drop by or call to check tour times. Learn why Yankee Doodle "stuck a feather in his cap and called it macaroni," and much more. Open daily 9:30 a.m. to 6:00 p.m., tel. 0225/61111.

▲▲Royal Crescent and The Circus—Bath is an architectural chorus line and these are the stars. These

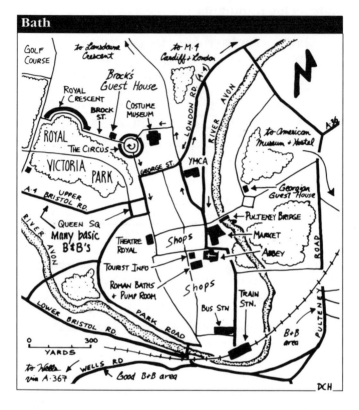

Bath

first elegant Georgian (that's British for "neoclassical")
"condos" by John Wood are well reviewed in the city
walking tours. The corner house at 1 Royal Crescent is
your best look into a house from Jane Austen's day. Worth
the £2 admission to get behind all those classy exteriors.
Tuesday through Saturday 11:00 a.m. to 5:00 p.m., Sunday
2:00 p.m. to 5:00 p.m., March through December only
(closed Monday).

National Centre of Photography—This is the only
museum of its kind I've seen, exhibiting the earliest
cameras and photos and their development along with
temporary contemporary exhibits. (Daily 10:00 a.m. to
6:00 p.m., closed Sundays, £2.)

▲**American Museum**—For years I shied away from this

place. I figured I needed it like I needed a Big Mac. On the
insistence of a friend, I went, and it's great—like nothing
I've seen at home. Each of 18 completely furnished rooms
from the 1600s to the 1800s is hosted by an eager guide
waiting to fill you in on the candles, maps, bedpans, and
various religious sects that make domestic Yankee history
surprisingly interesting. One room is a quilter's nirvana.
Open Tuesday through Saturday, 2:00 p.m. to 5:00 p.m.,
Sunday 11:00 a.m. to 5:00 p.m., April through October. A
special museum-bound round-trip bus (#25) leaves Bath
daily at 2:00 p.m., returning at 4:30. Entrance, £3.50.
The Abbey—On the main square, this is worth a look.
The Abbey is 500 years old, has good fan vaulting, and is
most impressive during an evensong service (schedule on
the door).

To best enjoy a sunny Bath kind of day, pay 50p to go
into the garden below the Pulteney Bridge. If the
weather's not great, enjoy a coffee with an elegant view
from David's Coffee Shop on Pulteney Bridge.

Food and Accommodations

Although it's one of England's most popular cities, Bath
handles its crowds well. The TI (tel. 0225/462831, open
Monday through Saturday 9:30 a.m. to 8:00 p.m., Sunday
10:00 a.m. to 6:00 p.m., shorter hours off-season,
24-hour computer information, pick up the cheap little
Bath map/guide) will find you a £12 to £15 B&B. Midday
arrivals should find a room, but this is a place for which I
would call ahead, especially in peak season.

Brock's Guest House: If you can afford the splurge,
this place is the "cherry on the top" of your Bath visit.
Marion Dodd just redid her place, built in 1765 by John
Wood. It's quiet and friendly and couldn't be better
located, between the Royal Crescent and the elegant Circle (moderate/expensive, 32 Brock St., tel. 0225/338374).
Marion serves a royal breakfast. TV and teapots in the
room, laundromat around the corner. Like nearly every
listing in this book, she'll hold telephone reservations

with no deposit until 5:00 p.m. (call if you'll be a little late). If Marion is full, she can set you up in a friend's B&B nearby.

The Bathurst Guest House: Mrs. Elizabeth Tovey runs another fine B&B (moderate, 11 Walcot Parade, London Road, Bath BA1-5NF, tel. 0225/21884) with a great lounge, no smoking, one block above the A-4 London Road about a 15-minute walk north of the town center.

The Georgian Guest House: Run by Sybil Barry, this is one of those tall, skinny places—lots of stairs. It's quiet, clean, very central, and (for Bath) reasonable, with breakfast and nothing- special rooms (moderate, 34 Henrietta St., Bath, BA2 6LR, tel. 424103).

The Claremont B&B (moderate, 9 Claremont Rd., Bath, 0225/28859): Mr. and Mrs. Long serve breakfast in a solarium overlooking the garden.

For the cheapest beds, the **Youth Hostel**, tel. 65674, is very nice but not central. The **YMCA**, tel. 60471, is a bit grungy but friendly and wonderfully central on Broad Street. Doubles are £9 per person; the dorm is cheaper at about £10.

Eating in Bath is fun. There's no shortage of places in all price ranges—just stroll around the center of town. I've enjoyed many meals in Bath simply by strolling until I found a place that tickled my fancy that evening. A picnic dinner in the Royal Crescent Park is ideal for aristocratic hobos.

For lunch, try the café upstairs in the **Bartlett Street Antique Centre** (downhill from the Assembly Rooms), or the **Crystal Palace Pub** with hearty meals under rustic timbers or in the sunny courtyard (inexpensive, just south of the Abbey at 11 Abbey Green, tel. 23944, children welcome on the patio).

Sally Lunn's House (4 North Parade Passage, Monday through Saturday 10:00 a.m. to 6:00 p.m., Sunday 12:00 noon to 6:00 p.m.) is a cutesy historic place for doily meals, tea, pink pillows, and lots of lace. It is the proud original home of the famous "Bath bun."

The Huntsman (next to Sally Lunn's on North Parade,

tel. 60100) offers several different places to eat good, filling meals. The pub is cheapest, the Cellar Bar is inexpensive and full of young locals. Consider eating in the restaurant upstairs (moderate and good view).

The Vendage Wine Bar (at 11 Margaret's Building, on a pedestrian alley just off Brock St., around the corner from the recommended Brock House B&B, between the Crescent and the Circus) is friendly and serves fine, moderately priced lunches and dinners daily. A most pleasant way to get your clothes washed is to use the laundromat across the street while you eat, or just sip wine while your knickers spin.

The Broad Street Bakery (14 Broad St.) is a budgetricious place with great quiches and pizzas to eat in or take away. The **Old Bond Street Restaurant** (14 Old Bond St.) has slow service but good, reasonably priced hot lunches.

Helpful Hints
Don't take the cleverly advertised but disappointing ghost walk. There's great shopping between the abbey and the Assembly Rooms, especially the many antique shops. The "walk and ride" tours are not as good as the free city walks. When in need, the Pump Room's toilets are always nearby and open to the discreet public. Shops close at 5:30 p.m., later on Thursdays.

WELLS, GLASTONBURY, WOOKEY HOLE

Today, after a free morning in Bath, swing south to visit Wells, England's smallest cathedral city; Glastonbury, steeped in legends of the Holy Grail and King Arthur; and the impressive—if a bit silly—haunted caves of Wookey Hole.

Suggested Schedule

Morning	Free in Bath.
1:00	Drive to Wookey Hole.
1:30	Tour Wookey Hole.
4:00	Browse around Wells town and cathedral, staying for the 5:15 evensong service.
6:00	Drive five miles to Glastonbury. Tour the abbey, then climb the tower before sun sets. Great view and creepy-crawly feelings.
8:00	Drive back to Bath, possibly stopping at a countryside pub for dinner.

Transportation: Bath to Wookey Hole and Wells (20 mi.) to Glastonbury (6 mi.) to Bath (26 mi.).
This plan calls for 50 miles of driving. The roads are good, the scenery okay but not earthshaking. I'd stick to the faster "A" roads, going as directly as possible.

In Wells, try to park on the main square next to the tourist office, post office, and just about everything else. In Glastonbury, the abbey parking lot is easy to find.

Sightseeing Highlights
▲**Wookey Hole**—This is definitely a commercial venture. It's a bit tacky but I think worth the £3 admission for two hours of fun. Just two miles from Wells, Wookey Hole is a hodgepodge of entertainment starting with a wookey guided tour of some big but mediocre caves complete with history, geology lessons, and witch stories. Then you're free to wander through a traditional rag papermaking mill with a demonstration, and into a

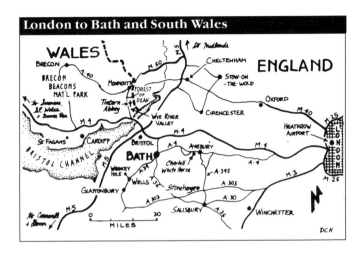

London to Bath and South Wales

nineteenth-century circus room—a riot of color, funny
mirrors, and a roomful of old penny arcade machines that
visitors can actually play for as long as their pennies (on
sale there) last. They even have old girlie shows. Finally
you come to Madame Tussaud's Cabinet of Curiosities,
which re-creates her traveling wax show from 1832.
(Open daily May through September, 9:30 a.m. to 5:30
p.m., October through April 10:30 a.m. to 4:30 p.m., tel.
0749/72243.)

▲▲ **Wells**—This wonderfully preserved little town has a
cathedral, so it can be called a city. Its thirteenth-century
cathedral is one of England's most interesting. Don't miss
the carving on the west front, the unique hourglass-shaped
double arch, the grand chapter house, or the nearby
bishop's palace (which is open Thursday and Sunday 2:00
p.m. to 6:00 p.m., daily in August, £2.50). The cathedral
(open daily, long hours) has a good shop and a handy cafeteria. Weekdays (except Wednesday) at 5:15 and Sundays
at 3:00 p.m., the cathedral choir gives a lovely 30-minute
evensong service.

If you're in the mood for a picnic, drop by the aromatic
Cheese Board on the market square for a great selection
of tasty local cheeses. Remember, Cheddar is just down
the road. Ask the lady for the most interesting mix worth

a pound. The Wells TI is on the Main Square (tel.
0749/72552).

▲▲**Glastonbury**—This place bubbles with legend and
history. Its once grand, now ruined abbey is the sup-
posed birthplace of Christianity in England. Five hundred years ago it was England's leading abbey. It's well
worth a wander. The little abbey museum has an impressive reconstruction of the abbey as it was before Henry
VIII destroyed it. The Glastonbury Tor is a conical hill,
supposedly the mystical Isle of Avalon from King Arthur's
day. You can drive around the hill and park very close to
its base. Hike to the summit for a marvelous view and a
great "king of the mountain" feeling. The abbey is open
daily until 6:30 p.m. The tower never closes. (TI tel.
0458/32954)

Itinerary Options
If you want to see the American Museum near Bath, which
is open only from 2:00 p.m. to 5:00 p.m., rearrange Day 6
by skipping your free time in Bath and the evensong service in Wells, doing Glastonbury first, then Wells and
Wookey Hole, arriving in Claverton outside of Bath by
3:00 p.m. to see the American Museum. Or you could follow the original schedule but replace Wookey Hole
with the American Museum, getting there right at 2:00 p.m.

Wells is so pleasant you might decide to spend the
night. The Tor Guest House, in a seventeenth-century
building facing the east end of the cathedral, is a good
value (inexpensive, cozy lounge and breakfast room,
quiet, friendly, with car park, 20 Tor St., BA5-2US, tel.
0749/72322). The nearby Fountain Inn, on St. Thomas
Street, is the best place for pub grub (fine curry, spare
ribs, and draft cider).

SOUTH WALES, FOLK MUSEUM, WYE RIVER VALLEY

From Bath, dash into South Wales past its capital city of Cardiff to spend the morning exploring the traditional past at St. Fagan's Welsh Folk Museum. Then take the scenic route past the romantic Tintern Abbey ruins, up the lush Wye River Valley, through the remote and quirky Forest of Dean, and into England's land of quaint—the Cotswold Hills—establishing your headquarters in the centrally situated village of Stow-on-the-Wold.

Suggested Schedule

8:00	Breakfast.
8:30	Drive to Cardiff.
10:00	St. Fagan's Welsh Folk Museum. Tour the grounds first, picnic, or lunch in cafeteria, then tour the museum gallery.
1:00	Drive to Tintern Abbey.
2:00	Explore Tintern, the Wye River, and the Forest of Dean.
5:00	Drive to Stow-on-the-Wold.
6:30	Set up in Stow.

Transportation: Bath to Cardiff (50 mi.) to Tintern (40 mi.) to Stow (60 mi.)
Bath—Cardiff, St. Fagan's: From Bath, it's 10 miles north on A46 past a village called Pennsylvania to the M4 super freeway. Now, only a speed reader can follow the map as you zip westward, crossing a huge suspension bridge into Wales. Twenty miles farther, just past Cardiff, take exit 33 and follow the brown signs south to the Welsh Folk Museum.

   Cardiff—Stow: From St. Fagan's, get back on the M4 as soon as possible and backtrack to just before the big suspension bridge. Take the Chepstow exit (22) and follow the signs up A466 to Tintern Abbey and the Wye River Valley. If you stop at the Tintern Abbey, buy the

Wye River-Cotswold Hills map. Carry on to Monmouth
and, if you're running late, follow the A40 and the M50 to
the Tewksebury exit, where the A438 and the B4077 will
zip you right into Stow-on-the-Wold.

   If you have time and energy, explore the romantic old
Forest of Dean (pick up information at the Tintern TI),
leaving the A466 for Coleford following the green shaded
"scenic routes" through the beloved old oak forest that
made Admiral Nelson's ships so strong. From Cinderford,
take the A48 and A40 through Cheltenham to Northleach,
from which it's a straight ten-minute shot on A429 to
Stow.

Sightseeing Highlights
▲**Cardiff**—The Welsh capital with 300,000 people and a
pleasant modern center across from the castle. The castle
visit is especially interesting if you catch one of the entertaining tours, which leave every half hour. The interior is
a Victorian fantasy.

▲▲▲**Welsh Folk Museum at St. Fagan's**—This is your
best look at traditional Welsh folk life. More than 20 old
houses from all corners of this little country have been
saved and reconstructed here. Each is fully furnished and
comes equipped with a local expert warming himself or
herself by the toasty fire and happy to tell you anything
you want to know about life in this old cottage. Ask questions! You'll also see traditional crafts in action and a fascinating gallery displaying crude washing machines, the
earliest matches, elaborately carved "love spoons," and
even a case of memorabilia from the local man who
pioneered cremation. Everything is well explained.
Museum admission is £3.50. Open daily 10:00 a.m. to
5:00 p.m., closed Sunday in the off-season (tel. 569441).

   There are three sections: houses, museum, and castle/
garden. If the sky's dry, I'd do the 20 old houses first for
60 to 90 minutes, spend an hour in the large building's
fascinating museum, skip the castle and gardens, and eat
lunch in the museum's excellent, inexpensive cafeteria,
called the Vale Restaurant.

▲**Caerphilly Castle**—This impressive but gutted old castle, only 30 minutes from the Welsh Folk Museum, is the second largest in Europe. (Windsor is the largest.) It has two concentric walls and was considered to be a brilliant arrangement of defensive walls and moats. It's interesting to see how Cromwell's demolition crew tried to destroy it, creating the leaning tower of Caerphilly. Open daily 9:30 a.m. to 6:00 p.m. (Note: this 22-day tour covers other equally impressive fortresses, so I'd skip this one to make time for the scenic drive to Stow.)

▲**Tintern Abbey**—Just off the scenic A466 road in a lush natural setting, this is worth a stop. The abbey shop and local tourist information desk next door are very helpful. You can buy the Wye-Cotswolds map and Wales Tourist Board's "A Tourist Guide to North Wales" here. Open daily.

▲**Wye River Valley and Forest of Dean**—Lush, mellow, and historic, this region seduced me into an unexpected overnight. Local tourist brochures explain the Forest of Dean's special dialect, strange political autonomy, and its ties to Trafalgar and Admiral Nelson.

Sightseeing Option: To make today possible, you must choose among the city of Cardiff, the Caerphilly castle, and the Tintern Abbey. Mortal travelers cannot fit more into a sane day.

Accommodations

Stow-on-the-Wold is the ideal home base for the Cotswolds. Although it has its crowds, most are comprised of day-trippers, so even summer nights are peaceful. Stow has plenty of B&B options and a tourist office (tel. 0451/31082) in Talbot Court, off the main square, which can find you a room. Here are some specifics:

The Croyde B&B: Norman and Barbara Axon make you feel like part of the family. Only after an hour of tea and talk did I have a chance to actually bring in my bag. They offer two doubles in a pleasant, quiet, modern house with a garden and easy parking (inexpensive-moderate, two blocks out of town on Evesham Rd., Stow-on-the-Wold, Nr. Cheltenham, Glos., GL54 1EJ, tel. 0451/31711). They can usually find a good bed for you if they're full.

West Deyne B&B: Mrs. Joan Cave runs this very cozy B&B. It's a three-minute walk out of town on Lower Swell Road, with a view and a garden (inexpensive-moderate, GL54-1LD, tel. 0451/31011).

The Pound: Comfy, quaint, restored 500-year-old low-ceilinged, heavy-beamed home of Patricia White-head (moderate, right downtown on Sheep St. GL54 1AU, tel. 30229).

The Limes (moderate, a short walk from town on Evesham Rd., tel. 0451/30034) is friendly, has a nice garden, and serves a great breakfast.

The Guest House: Six miles west of Stow in the tiny village of Guiting Power, this is your sleepy-village alternative. Modern, clean, and friendly, in a 400-year-old house (moderate, Post Office Lane, Guiting Power, Cheltenham, GL545TZ, tel. 0451/850-470). If you're just passing through, drop in for a lovely afternoon cream tea.

Camden Pottery B&B: In my second favorite Cotswold home base, Chipping Camden, the B&B is a fine value (0386/840315).

Stow-on-the-Wold Youth Hostel: Right on the main square of Stow in a historic old building, well run, friendly atmosphere, good hot meals served and a do-it-yourself member's kitchen, popular in summer. Call-in reservations (tel. 0451/30497) are held until 6:00 p.m., or later with a credit card number. £4 per bed, £2.50 for dinner. Rental bikes available.

Other Cotswold Youth Hostels: The hostels at Cleve Hill (tel. 024267/2065), Duntisbourne Abbots (tel. 028582/682), and Charlbury (tel. 0608/810202) are good bases for exploring the Cotswold villages. Each rents bikes for £2 per day. Call 05432/22279 for specifics.

Eating in Stow
The bar in the **Stow Lodge** serves great food at moderate prices. The **Queen's Head**, on the main square, serves an

inexpensive decent meal. Try their local Cotswold brew, Donnington. The cheapest meal in town is at the hostel (7:00 p.m.). For a good dinner, drive ten minutes to Upper Oddington and a pub called **Horse and Groom**. You'll find hearty, tasty food, a great local crowd, memorable Taunton Blackthorn dry cider, and special homemade ice cream.

For a pleasant 1½-mile walk to real ale and good food, walk to the **Fox Pub** in Broadwell.

Itinerary Options

If you want to skip the scenic three hours of Tintern, Wye, and Dean, you could spend an hour in Cardiff and an hour at the Caerphilly Castle, and take the Motorway (M4, M5) and A436 direct to Stow. Or, if you stepped up the tempo throughout, adding just a tinge of hecticity to the plan, you could sneak Caerphilly Castle into the suggested itinerary after St. Fagan's. If you need to save a day somewhere, consider skipping South Wales entirely.

For a medieval night, check into the St. Briavals Castle Youth Hostel (cheap, tel. 0594/530272, you must be a Youth Hostel member). It's an 800-year-old Norman castle used by King John in 1215, the year he signed the Magna Carta, comfortable (as castles go), friendly, and in the center of the quiet village of St. Briavels just north of Tintern Abbey. For dinner, eat at the hostel or walk "just down the path and up the snyket" to the Crown Pub (very friendly, with good, cheap food and fine pub atmosphere).

If a restful seaside break sounds good about now, consider a side trip to Gower Peninsula (southwest of Swansea, about a 90-minute drive from Cardiff) for a pleasant blend of farms, ancient monuments, sleepy towns, cliffs, and windswept Welsh beaches. Head straight for rugged Rhossili town on the western tip of the peninsula. Among several fine hikes in the area, one takes you high above the beach with great views and an opportunity to frolic with the spirit of Dylan Thomas among the lush hillsides and peaceful ponies. Rhossili has one hotel (Worms Head, tel. 0792/390512) and several B&Bs.

THE COTSWOLD VILLAGES AND BLENHEIM PALACE

Today mixes England's coziest villages with her greatest countryside palace. The Cotswold Hills are dotted with storybook villages. The best are within easy reach of Stow-on-the-Wold. England has plenty of royal country mansions. If you had to choose just one to visit, Blenheim would be it.

Suggested Schedule

8:00	Breakfast in Stow-on-the-Wold.
8:30	Drive to Chipping Campden.
9:00	Joyride through Chipping Campden, Broadway, and Stanton, then drive via Cheltenham to Cirencester (park in central lot).
11:00	Cirencester—Corinium Museum, crafts center, lunch in crafts center cafeteria.
1:00	Drive to Bibury via Coln St. Dennis, Coln Rogers, and Winson.
1:30	Bibury—stroll along the stream, see cottages and church.
2:30	Drive to Blenheim via Burford, Witney, and Woodstock (on A4095).
3:15	Park at palace and line up for the hour-long tour of Blenheim Palace.
5:15	Drive to Stow-on-the-Wold via Chipping Norton.
6:00	Evening stroll around Stow center. Find a good pub for dinner.

The Cotswolds

As with many fairy tale regions of Europe, the present-day beauty of the Cotswolds was the result of an economic disaster. The area grew rich on the wool trade and built lovely towns and houses. Then foreign markets stole their trade and they slumped—too poor even to be knocked down. The forgotten, time-passed villages have been rediscovered by us twentieth-century romantics, and the Cotswold villages are enjoying new prosperity.

Transportation

Although distances are very small in the Cotswolds, so are the roads. Including the 20-mile drive to Blenheim, you'll probably put in 100 miles today—most of it as joyful as joyriding can be. Don't bumble around without a good map; any shop can sell you a fine, tourist-oriented map of the region. Peak season parking in Broadway and Bourton is a headache. Blenheim Palace is in the town of Woodstock on A34, seven miles northwest of Oxford. The palace turnoff is right in the town, not well signposted. By the way, a "quick swing into Oxford" won't work: it has the worst traffic and parking problems in England. Today's theme is cuteness, and the best way to quench your thirst for cuteness is to take the tiny roads.

Sightseeing Highlights

▲**Stow-on-the-Wold**—Eight roads converge on Stow, but none interrupt the peacefulness of its main square. The town has no real sights other than itself. There are several good pubs, some pleasant shops, and a handy little walking tour brochure called "Town Trail" (15p, sold at the TI and at the Youth Hostel counter). Try out the stocks on the green.

▲**Cirencester**—1,800 years ago, this was the ancient Roman city of Corinium. It's 20 miles from Stow down A429, which was called Foss Way in Roman times. In Cirencester (towns ending in "cester" were Roman camps), don't miss the Corinium Museum (open 10:00 a.m. to 6:00 p.m., Sunday 2:00 p.m. to 6:00 p.m.) to find out why they say, "If you scratch Gloucestershire, you'll find Rome." The craft center and workshops entertain visitors with traditional weaving, baking, and potting in action. You could also visit an interesting gallery and a great cafeteria. Friday is market day in Cirencester.

Cotswold Farming and Prison Museum—Nine miles south of Stow, just off the Foss Way (A429) at Northleach.

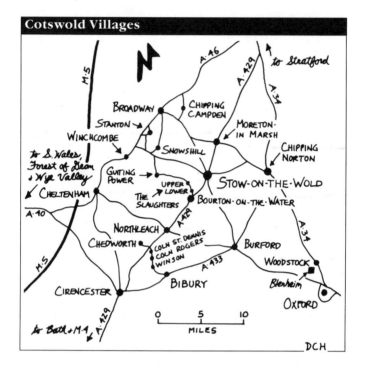

Cotswold Villages

Worthwhile only if you're interested in old farming machines. (No crowd problems—ever.)

   Bourton-on-the-Water—I can't figure out if they call this the "Venice of the Cotswolds" because of its quaint canals, its miserable crowds, or just to make more money. It's too cute, worth a drive through but no more; four miles south of Stow.

Broadway—Another very crowded town, worth a drive through but not a stop. There won't be a parking place anyway; nine miles northwest of Stow.

   ▲▲**Chipping Campden**—This is a close second to Stow for the best home base. Nine miles north of Stow, it's a real working market town, home of some incredibly beautiful thatched roofs and the richest Cotswold wool merchants ("Cotswold" comes from the Saxon phrase meaning "hills of sheeps' coats"). Pleasant for a walk.

   ▲▲**Snowshill and Stanton**—Both are two miles south

of Broadway. These two towns, along with Upper and
Lower Slaughter (three miles south of Stow), are my
nominations for the cutest Cotswold villages. They're
almost edible, each nestled in equally beautiful countryside.

▲**Bibury**—Six miles northeast of Cirencester, this is an
entertaining, but not very friendly, village with a trout
farm, a Cotswolds museum, a stream thriving with fat
trout and proud ducks, a row of very old weavers' cottages, and a church surrounded by rose bushes, each
tended by a volunteer of the parish. Don't miss the scenic
drive from Bibury to A429 through the villages of Win-
son, Coln St. Dennis, and Coln Rogers. Drivers might
consider skipping Cirencester, dropping passengers in
Coln Rogers for a pleasant walk (two miles) into Bibury
where they, devoted drivers, will have an idyllic stream-
bank picnic awaiting the walkers.

▲▲▲**Blenheim Palace**—It's easy to O.D. on English
palaces, so this tour chooses just the best. The Duke of
Marlborough's home, the largest in England, is still lived
in. That is wonderfully obvious as you tour it. Churchill
was born prematurely while his mother was at a Blenheim Palace party (truly a man before his time). The palace is well organized with mandatory, excellent guided
tours that leave every ten minutes, last an hour, and cost
£4. There's an excellent new Churchill exhibit that is
worth lingering over, so skip to the next tour group if you
need more time here. The palace is open from March
through October, 10:30 a.m. to 5:30 p.m.; last tour leaves
at 5:00 p.m. Churchill fans can visit his tomb in a nearby
town.

▲**Woodstock**—Blenheim Palace sits at the edge of this
cute town, stealing the show. For a half-timbered and
memorable splurge, the Star Inn (expensive, Market Place,
tel. 0993/811373) is good for an overnight.

▲**Hidcote Manor**—If you like gardens, the grounds
around this manor house are worth a look. These
gardens, among the best in England, are at their best in
May, June, and July. (£3.50 open 11:00 to 5:30, just past
Chipping Campden.)

Itinerary Options

For a more leisurely day, skip Chipping Campden and
Broadway and check out Upper and Lower Slaughter and
Bourton-on-the-Water as you drive down to Cirencester.
You could drive through Chipping Campden and Broadway on your way to Stratford tomorrow morning. Remember, you're just 30 minutes from Stratford, Shakespeare's
birthplace. The world's best Shakespeare is performed by
the Royal Shakespeare Company there and in London.
You'll probably need to get your tickets in advance (in
London on the first day of your trip). It would be a
worthwhile pilgrimage if you're a Shakespeare fan.

If you'd prefer Oxford to Cambridge (which is reasonable, though I don't), you can do it as a side trip from
London or from Stow-on-the-Wold. Consider an extra
day in the itinerary here, which would give you a whole
day in the Cotswolds and a day split between Blenheim
and Oxford (11:00 a.m. Blenheim tour, in Oxford by 1:00
p.m.; go straight to the tourist office to reserve a spot on
an afternoon city walking tour).

Consider renting a bike for a more intimate look at the
Cotswolds where, according to some, two hours on two
wheels is worth two days on four. The Stow youth hostel
and Teagues in Bourton-on-the-Water (High St., tel.
20248) rent bikes for 75p per hour. The Slaughters are a
fun bike ride away. Plan a picnic.

STRATFORD-UPON-AVON, WARWICK CASTLE, AND COVENTRY CATHEDRAL TO IRONBRIDGE GORGE

Today's drive into the cradle of the Industrial Revolution is a hopscotch of interesting sights. Spend the morning touring Shakespeare's birthplace at Stratford. Explore England's greatest medieval castle in Warwick, then visit Coventry and its cathedral, the symbol of the destruction of World War II, the determination to rebuild, and the hope for peace and reconciliation. Finally, zoom (hopefully) through England's second largest city, Birmingham, and into the Severn River valley, once churning with industry and now a land of sleepy smokestacks, soothing natural beauty, and a distinct Shropshire brand of hospitality.

Suggested Schedule

8:30	Leave Stow-on-the-Wold.
9:15	Park in Stratford.
9:30	See the "World of Shakespeare" show.
10:00	Walk around town, visit Shakespeare's house.
11:30	Drive to Warwick, picnic at the castle.
12:30	Tour the castle.
2:30	Drive to Coventry.
2:45	Tour new and old Cathedral, visitor's center, and wander around Coventry.
5:00	Drive to Ironbridge Gorge.
6:30	Arrive in Ironbridge Gorge.

Transportation: Stow to Stratford (20 mi.) to Warwick (8 mi.) to Coventry (10 mi.) to Ironbridge (56 mi.)
Today's sights are close together and served by fine roads. Drive directly from one stop to the next. From Stow, drive 20 miles north on A429 and A34 to Stratford. In Stratford, cross the bridge and you're in the center. Take the immediate left and park as close to the bridge as you can.

It's only eight miles to Warwick along A46. The castle is well signposted, just south of town to the right of the main road. After Warwick, follow the signs to Coventry (still on A46), and in Coventry follow signs to the "city centre" and then to the "cathedral." The cathedral is hard to see, so just look for signs or the reddish spires within the central ring road. When you get to what looks like a large bus station, park in the high-rise "cathedral car park."

From the cathedral, follow signs through lots of sprawl to the M6 and you're on your way. The M6 threads through giant Birmingham. This plan hits rush hour, but it doesn't seem to be a problem. From M6, take the new M54 to the Telford/Ironbridge exit. Following the Iron-bridge signs, you do-si-do through a long series of roundabouts until you're there. Public transportation around Ironbridge is confusing but workable. Call 0345/056785 for help.

Sightseeing Highlights

▲ **Stratford-upon-Avon**—This is the most overrated tourist magnet in England, but you're passing through, and nobody back home would understand if you skipped Shakespeare's house.

Shakespeare's hometown is blanketed with opportunities for "bardolotry." Only his birthplace on Henley Street is worth a visit on this itinerary. You'll enter through a modern Shakespeare Centre that has little to offer besides some fine BBC theater costumes, clean toilets, and a high-tech cash register, which from 9:00 a.m. to 6:00: p.m. daily will relieve you of £2.

The World of Shakespeare, gimmicky but fun, shows on the half hour (25 minutes, £2.25) and is located between the big Theatre and the bridge in the Heritage Theatre.

If you need a clean, friendly B&B in Stratford, try Pam and David Newberry's Carlton Guest House (inexpensive-moderate, 22 Evesham Place, CV37 6HT, tel. 0789/293548).

▲▲ **Royal Shakespeare Company**—The RSC, undoubtedly the best Shakespeare Company on earth, splits its season between London and Stratford. If you're

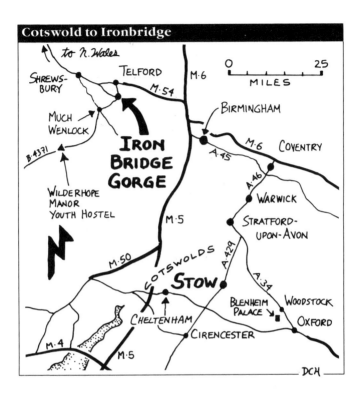

Cotswold to Ironbridge

to n. Wales
SHREWS-BURY
TELFORD
M·6
MUCH WENLOCK
M·54
BIRMINGHAM
B·4371
WILDERHOPE MANOR YOUTH HOSTEL
IRON BRIDGE GORGE
COVENTRY
M·6
A·45
A·46
WARWICK
STRATFORD-UPON-AVON
M·5
N
M·50
COTSWOLDS
A·429
A·34
STOW
BLENHEIM PALACE
WOODSTOCK
CHELTENHAM
OXFORD
CIRENCESTER
M·4
M·5
O ⸻ 25
MILES
DCH

a Shakespeare fan, see if the RSC schedule works into
your itinerary while you're in London at the start of your
trip. It's easy to make a Stratford show from Stow-on-the-
Wold, or in London before you fly home. You'll probably
need to buy your tickets in advance (although 50 seats are
saved to be sold each morning, and unclaimed tickets can
often be picked up the evening of the show; box office
tel. 0789/295623, information tel. 0789/69191).

▲▲**Warwick Castle**—England's finest medieval castle is
almost too groomed and organized, giving its hordes of
visitors a good value for the steep £5 entry fee. Situated
above a different Avon River with a lush green grassy
moat and fairy tale fortification, Warwick will entertain
you from dungeon to lookout. There's something for
every taste—a fine and educational armory, a terrible tor-

ture chamber, a knight in shining armor posing on a
horse, a Madame Tussaud re-creation of a royal weekend
party with an 1898 game of statue-maker, and a grand garden and peacock-patrolled, picnic-perfect park. (Open
daily 10:00 a.m. to 5:30 p.m.)

▲▲**Coventry's Cathedral**—The Germans bombed
Coventry to smithereens in 1940. From that point on,
their word for "to really blast the heck out of a place" was
to "coventrate." But Coventry left smithereens, and its
message to our world is one of forgiveness and reconciliation. The symbol of Coventry is the bombed-out hulk
of its old cathedral with the brilliant new one adjoining
it. The complex welcomes visitors. Climb the tower, pick
up a guided walk brochure, savor the powerful modern
art, search for the symbolism, ask a hostess about the
Community of the Cross of Nails, see the visitors center
(£1.25 donation to the church, daily 9:30 a.m. to 5:00
p.m., Sunday 11:30 a.m. to 3:30 p.m.) with its award-
winning 18-minute movie, *The Spirit of Coventry.* Have
tea and scones or a light lunch in the cafeteria.

Also of interest in Coventry: within a block or two of
the cathedral (near Broadgate) is a bronze statue of
Coventry's most famous hometown girl, Lady Godiva,
who rode bareback through the town in the eleventh
century to help lower taxes, and the Museum of British
Road Transport (first, fastest, and most famous cars and
motorcycles from this British "Detroit").

Accommodations and Food
The Ironbridge Gorge is a young attraction and doesn't
have a lot of accommodations, but these are good:

The Hill View Farm—John and Rosemarie Hawkins
run a peaceful, clean, friendly farmhouse B&B in a great
rural setting overlooking the ruins of an old abbey. A real
value (inexpensive, Buildwas, Ironbridge, Shropshire,
TF8 7BP; tel. 2228), it's located halfway between Ironbridge and Much Wenlock; leave Ironbridge past the
huge modern power plants (coal, not nuclear, but omi-
nous nonetheless), cross the bridge, and go about a mile.
You'll see the sign.

Wilderhope Manor Youth Hostel—The beautifully remote and haunted 500-year-old manor house is one of my favorite youth hostels anywhere in Europe. One day a week, tourists actually pay to see what we youth hostelers sleep in for £4. Six and a half miles from Much Wenlock down B4371 toward Church Stretton. Tel. 06943/363. Evening meal served at 7:00 p.m.

Ironbridge Gorge Youth Hostel—Built in 1859 as the Coalbrookdale Institute, this grand hostel is a 20-minute walk from the Ironbridge, down A4169 toward Wellington. Tel. 095245/3281. They'll hold a room if you call and leave a credit card number.

Other inexpensive B&Bs in Ironbridge Gorge: Mrs. Reed's **Severn Lodge** (New Road, Ironbridge, Shropshire, TF87AX, tel. 2148), Mrs. Roberts's **Woodland Grange** (48 Lincoln Hill, tel. 2309), Mrs. Bowdler's **Vine Cottage** (45 Lincoln Hill, tel. 3767), Mrs. Pearce's **The Grove** (New Road, tel. 3218), Mrs. Gilbride's **Paradise House** (Coalbrookdale, tel. 3379), Mrs. Tyley's **Wren's Nest Cottage** (45 Newbridge Road, tel. 3061), and Mrs. Hedges's **Bridge House** (Buildwas, Ironbridge, tel. 2105). The **Tontine Hotel** (moderate, directly across from the Iron Bridge, tel. 095245/2127) is the only hotel in town—basic, brick, old, and musty, like its town.

For a pleasant evening, drive down Wenlock Edge on B4371. At Wenlock Edge Inn, park and walk to the cliff for a marvelous view of Shropshire at sunset. For dinner, drive 4 miles farther to Cardington and eat at the **Royal Oak** pub. This is a real country pub with good meals. Also good in the area for dinner are the **George and Dragon Pub** and the **Talbot Pub**, in Much Wenlock.

IRONBRIDGE GORGE MUSEUMS—NORTH WALES

Go from the gritty pits of England's industrial infancy to the poetic hills of remote northern Wales. The Industrial Revolution started in England's Severn River Valley. Today, the Ironbridge Gorge is preserved as a showcase of the days that boosted England into world leadership.

In its glory days, this now-drowsy valley gave the world the first iron wheels, steam-powered locomotive, and cast iron bridge and powered Britain to the pinnacle of the industrial world.

Suggested Schedule

8:30	Breakfast.
9:30	Iron Bridge, town, shops.
10:00	Visit the Museum of the River and Visitors' Centre, introduction video, exhibit.
11:00	Museum of Iron, Darby's furnace, Rosehill, Ironmaster's House (or go directly to Blists Hill).
12:00	Blists Hill Open-Air Museum, picnic, cafeteria or pub lunch.
3:30	Drive to Wales.
4:30	Llangollen, 30-minute stop in town or at abbey.
5:00	Horseshoe Pass Road to Ruthin.
6:00	Check into your Ruthin B&B.
7:30	Medieval Banquet at Ruthin Castle.
11:00	Find your way home.
12:00	Still not home? More mead!

Sightseeing Highlights—Ironbridge

▲▲▲ **Ironbridge Gorge Industrial Revolution Museums**—Start with the Iron Bridge. The first ever (1779), this is the area's centerpiece, open all the time and free.

The Museum of the River and Visitors' Centre, in the Severn Warehouse 500 yards upstream, is the orientation center. Be here at 10:00 a.m. when it opens to see the

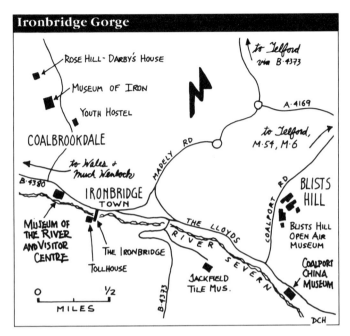

Ironbridge Gorge

ROSE HILL- DARBY'S HOUSE

MUSEUM OF IRON

YOUTH HOSTEL

COALBROOKDALE

to Wales & much Wenlock

B·4380

IRONBRIDGE
TOWN

MUSEUM OF
THE RIVER
AND VISITOR
CENTRE

THE IRONBRIDGE

TOLLHOUSE

0   ½
MILES

*to Telford
via B·4373*

A·4169

*to Telford,
M·54, M·6*

MADELY RD

THE LLOYDS

RIVER SEVERN

B·4373

JACKFIELD
TILE MUS.

COALPORT RD

BLISTS
HILL

BLISTS HILL
OPEN AIR
MUSEUM

COALPORT
CHINA
MUSEUM

DCH

introductory movie, check out its exhibit, and buy your
guidebook and tickets (£5.50 for the Ironbridge Passport
to all the sights, £4.20 for Blists Hill only).

Just up the road in Coalbrookdale are the Museum of
Iron (worth a quick look), Abraham Darby's blast furnace,
and a restored eighteenth-century ironmaster's house,
Rosehill. Here, in 1709, Darby first smelted iron using
coke as fuel. If you're like me, "coke" is a drink and
"smelt" is the past tense of smell, but this event kicked
off the modern industrial age.

Save most of your time and energy for the great Blists
Hill Open-Air Museum—50 acres of Victorian industry,
factories, and a re-created community from the 1890s
complete with Victorian chemists, an ancient dentist's
chair, candlemakers, a working pub, a fascinating squatter's cottage, and a snorty, slipslidey pigsty. Take the
lovely walk along the canal to the inclined plane, lunch in
the Victorian Pub, and have a picnic or pick up a very
light meal in the tearoom near the squatter's cottage. Buy

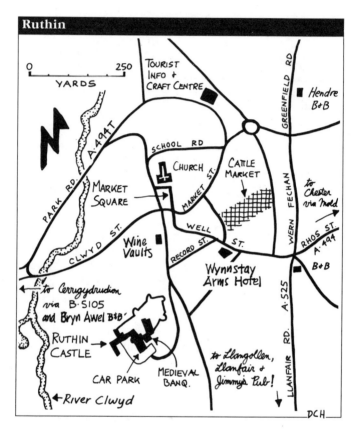

Ruthin

0 ——— 250
YARDS

TOURIST INFO + CRAFT CENTRE

GREENFIELD RD

Hendre B&B

A·494T

PARK RD.

SCHOOL RD

CHURCH

MARKET SQUARE

MARKET ST.

CATTLE MARKET

WERN FECHAN

to Chester via Mold

CLWYD ST.

WELL ST.

RHOS ST. A·494

Wine Vaults

RECORD ST.

Wynnstay Arms Hotel

B&B

A·525

to Cerrigydrudion via B·5105 and Bryn Awel B&B

RUTHIN CASTLE

CAR PARK

MEDIEVAL BANQ.

to Llangollen, Llanfair + Jimmy's Pub!

LLANFAIR RD.

River Clwyd

DCH

the guidebook for a good step-by-step rundown. Open 10:00 a.m. to 6:00 p.m. daily. Information tel. 095245/ 3522. In July and August there's a free shuttle bus between all sights; otherwise, those without wheels are in tough shape.

Transportation: Ironbridge to Ruthin, North Wales (60 mi.)

Most of the day is spent at easy-to-find museums within a few miles of the Iron Bridge. In midafternoon, drive for an hour to Wales via A458 through Shrewsbury, crossing into Wales at the pretty castle town of Chirk. There, take A5 to Llangollen. Cross the bridge in Llangollen, turn left, and follow A542 and A525 past the romantic Valle Crucis Abbey, over the scenic Horseshoe Pass, and into Ruthin.

Sightseeing Highlights—North Wales

▲**Llangollen**—Well worth a stop, Llangollen is famous for its International Eisteddfod (for a week starting the first Tuesday in July), a festival of folk songs and dance, very popular—and crowded. You can walk or ride a horse-drawn boat down its old canal (45 minutes round-trip, inexpensive) toward the lovely thirteenth-century Cistercian Abbey near the even older and more thought-provoking old cross called Eliseg's Pillar. You at least glimpse all these things from the A542 on your way up the exciting Horseshoe Pass road. TI tel. 0978/860828.

▲**Ruthin**—The ideal home base for your exploration of North Wales, Ruthin (pronounced "rith-in") is a market town serving the scenic Vale of Clwyd (pronounced "klu-id"). Each Wednesday is Medieval Day as the square dresses up and everything goes traditional (10:00 a.m. to 5:00 p.m. in summer from first of June). The Tourist Information Office (10:00 a.m. to 6:00 p.m. daily in summer, tel. 08242/3992) can give you plenty of information and book reservations for rooms and the medieval banquet. Located in a busy crafts center with 13 working shops, a gallery, and a fine cafeteria, the place bubbles with small-town community spirit.

▲▲**The Ruthin Castle Welsh Medieval Banquet**—By many accounts, this is Britain's best "medieval banquet." Of course, it's a touristy gimmick—but what a fun one. For one crazy evening, I chose to accept this romanti-cized trip into the bawdy Welsh past. English, Scottish, Irish, and Welsh medieval banquets are all variations on the same theme. This one is more tasteful and less expensive than most, and it plays right into our 22-day plan.

You start off with a chunk of bread dipped in salt which the maiden mentions will "guarantee your safety." Your medieval master of ceremonies then seats you, and the evening of food, drink, and music rolls gaily on. Harp music, angelic singing, wenches serving mead, spiced wine, four hearty traditional courses eaten with your fingers and a dagger, bibs, candlelight, pewter goblets, and lots of entertainment including insults slung at the Irish, Scots, English, and even us brash colonists.

The banquet costs £18, starts at 7:15 p.m. nearly every evening, and usually sells out (well in advance on Friday and Saturday evenings). Call in a reservation to 08242/3435. The castle is just down Castle Street from the town square, with easy parking at the doorstep. (Off-season banquets usually Thursday through Saturday, but call to check.)

Accommodations

Bryn Awel—Beryl and John Jones run a warm, traditional, charming, and inexpensive farmhouse B&B in the hamlet of Bontuchel just outside of Ruthin (tel. 08242/2481). Beryl is an excellent cook, eager to help you with touring tips and a few key Welsh words. She's happy to hold a room if you telephone her. She can call and reserve the medieval banquet for you. Take the B5105 Cerrigydrudion Road out of Ruthin. Turn right after the church, at the Bontuchel/Cyffylliog sign. Bryn Awel is on the right 1 mile down the little road. Go to the Bridge Hotel and backtrack 200 yards.

Eyarth Station—Jen and Bert Spencer run this modern, friendly B&B about a mile south of Ruthin. Remote scenic setting in former train station; a warm, friendly family atmosphere prevails. Jen is also very helpful with your travel plans. Take A525 (Wrexham Road) for about a mile. Take the first right, following the signs to Eyarth Station (moderate, Llanfair D.C., Ruthin, Clwyd, N. Wales LL15 2EE, tel. 08242/3643).

Wynnstay Arms Hotel—For budget rooms right in the center of Ruthin, consider this gangly, frumpy, old, down-home pub inn. Cromwell mounted his horse from a stone in the backyard. You're a three-minute walk from the castle, the food in the pub is good, the crowd is local and could keep a poet very busy, and the price is right.

Friendly, dark and creaky, some soggy beds (inexpensive-moderate, 20 Well St., tel. 08242/3147).

Hendre, run by friendly Mr. and Mrs. King, is close to town, small, modern, and clean. (Greenfield Rd., first left off the Mold Road from the roundabout near the TI, tel. 4078.) Next door is **Sally Price's B&B** (tel. 3847).

The Wine Vaults is an old inn right on Ruthin's main square, run by Mrs. Taylor, with a pub downstairs, most central location possible, great guests' lounge, modern plumbing. A little musty and less cozy than a B&B (moderate, tel. 2067).

The Ruthin Castle is the ultimate in Old World elegance for North Wales. Its doubles are worth the £60 they charge. Tel. 08242/2664. Dogs are welcome for a £2-a-night supplement.

McGregor's Pit B&B—If you don't mind unflushed toilets, dog hairs everywhere, an occasional old tampon in the corner, and windows boarded shut, call this place. Mr. McGregor keeps his house too warm but serves a cold breakfast and usually wants payment in advance (moderate, no telephone, no address).

The Holt Youth Hostel in Maeshafn on the Mold Road, seven miles out of Ruthin (cheap, Mold, Clwyd, CH7 5LR, tel. 035285/320) is open in summer only.

Food
Pub grub is the way to eat well, cheaply, and in good company in Ruthin. The **Anchor Pub**, a bit upscale and bright, has good food. The **Wynnstay Arms Bar** serves good dinners with lowbrow conversation for dessert. The **White Horse Inn** (in Llanfair Village, two miles south on A525) is a good pool-and-darts Welsh pub, even though Jimmy's gone. For a very tasty, reasonably priced meal in a rustic and historic pub, visit the **Cerrigllwy-dion Arms Pub** in Llanynys (two miles north of Ruthin, take A525 Denbigh, turn off at Rhewl, tel. 074/578-247). The cafeteria in the crafts center next to the TI is bright and cheery. The **Cross Keys Inn** is a friendly Ruthin pub

serving excellent meals. Also consider the **Manor House Hotel Restaurant** for a moderate dinner.

Itinerary Options
If you're not into heavy metal, leave the Ironbridge museums early after lunch (skip the Museum of Iron, doing just the Blist's Hill Museum) and take a scenic detour from Ironbridge south along Wenlock Edge (B4368) for the best Shropshire scenery. Use the 95p Shropshire guide available at any local tourist office. Drive from Clun, wind up to Welshpool, and from there go to Llangollen for a longer stop.

   If you can't do the medieval banquet tonight, try to book it for tomorrow. If you didn't buy the North Wales guide in South Wales, get it in Llangollen.

EXPLORING NORTH WALES

Today's sightseeing menu is a real Welsh stew: a tour of Caernarfon, North Wales' mightiest castle; one of the world's largest slate mines at Blaenau Ffestiniog; and some of Britain's most beautiful scenery in the Snowdonia National Park, driving around the towering Mount Snowdon through lush forests and desolate moor country.

Suggested Schedule

8:30	Breakfast (earlier if possible).
9:00	Drive to Caernarfon with short stops in Trefriw Mill, Betws-y-Coed (information center, shops, waterfalls), and over Llanberis Mountain Pass.
11:30	Arrive at Caernarfon, and picnic in the castle or on the waterfront.
12:00	Caernarfon Castle. Catch noon tour, 1:00 p.m. movie in Eagle Tower, 1:30 p.m. climb to top for view.
2:00	Walk through town, shop, see Regimental Museum or Prince Charles (of Wales) Exhibit in the castle.
2:30	Drive the scenic road to Blaenau Ffestiniog.
3:30	Tour Llechwedd Slate Mines.
5:30	Drive home via Denbigh.
7:00	Arrive back in Ruthin.

Transportation: Ruthin to Caernarfon (56 mi.) to Blaenau (34 mi.) to Ruthin (35 mi.)

Every road in North Wales has its charm, but this day includes the best—lots of scenic wandering on small roads. Take the little B5105 road out of Ruthin to Cerrigydrudion (down the steepest road off the main square and follow the signs to Cerrigydrudion). Then follow the A5 into Betws-y-Coed with a possible quick detour to the Trefriw Woollen Mill (three miles north on B5106, well signposted). At Chapel Curig, take A4086 over the rugged

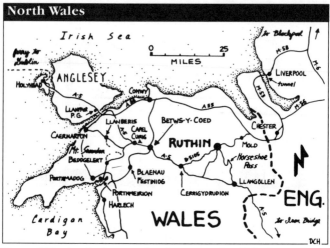

North Wales

Pass of Llanberis, just under the summit of Mt. Snowdon (to the south, behind those clouds), and on to Caernarfon. Park under the castle (very central) in the harborside car park.

The A4085 from Caernarfon southeast through Beddgelert to Penrhyndeudraeth is lovely. Make things even more beautiful by taking the little B4410 road from Garreg to Maentwrog. Go through the dark, depressing mining town of Blaenau Ffestiniog on A470 until you wind up into the hills of slate and turn right into the Llechwedd Slate Mine.

After the mine, A470 continues north into the most scenic stretch of all (past a ruined castle and several remote, intriguing B&Bs) through Dolwyddelan and back to A5, which you take for six miles east before following the windy, windy (curvy, blowy) A543 road over the stark moors to the Sportsmans Arms Pub (the highest pub in Wales, good food). From there, take the tiny road past Nantglyn back into Ruthin. Be warned: the traffic on the north coast route past Conwy is often miserable.

Sightseeing Highlights

Betws-y-Coed—This is the resort center of Snowdonia National Park, with more than its share of tour buses and souvenir shops. It has a good National Park and Tourist Information office (tel. 06902/426). The main street is worth a walk.

As you drive out of town on A5, you'll see the car park for the scenic Swallow Falls, a five-minute walk from the road. A mile or so past the falls, on the right, you'll see "The Ugly House," built overnight to take advantage of a fifteenth-century law that let any quickie building avoid fees and taxes.

Trefriw Woollen Mills—In Trefriw, two miles north of Betws-y-Coed, free, and surprisingly interesting (Monday through Friday 9:00 a.m. to 5:30 p.m., Saturday 10:00 a.m. to 4:00 p.m., Sunday in July and August 2:00 p.m. to 5:00 p.m., tel. 0492/640462). Follow the eleven stages of wool manufacturing—warping, weaving, carding, hanking, spinning, and so on; then enjoy the fine woollen shop, pleasant town (more so than Betws-y-Coed), and a coffee shop.

▲▲Caernarfon Castle—Edward I built this impressive castle 700 years ago to establish English rule over North Wales. It's a great castle, all ready to entertain. See the movie (on the half hour in the Eagle Tower), climb the Eagle Tower for a great view, take the guided tour (50-minute-long tours for 70p leave on the hour from the center of the courtyard in front of entry; if you are late, ask to join one in progress); see the special exhibit on the investiture of Prince Charles and earlier Princes of Wales (daily 9:30 a.m. to 6:30 p.m., Sunday 2:00 to 6:30, tel. 0286/77617, £3).

Caernarfon is a great town bustling with shops, cafes, and people. The TI across from the castle entrance (tel. 0286/6/2232) can nearly always find you an inexpensive B&B.

▲Llechwedd Slate Mine Tour—Slate mining played a huge role in the Welsh heritage and this mine on the north edge of the bleak mining town of Blaenau Ffestiniog does its best to explain the mining culture of Wales. This is basically a romanticized view of the depressing existence of the Welsh miners of the Victorian age who mined and split most of the slate roofs of Europe. For every ton of usable slate found, ten tons are mined. Wales has a poor economy, so touristizing slate mines is understandable. Open 10:00 a.m. to 5:00 p.m. daily, March 20 through October 31, two tours offered (the "deep mine" tour features the social life, the tramway focuses on the working life), £3.25 for one tour or £5 for both. Dress warmly and don't miss the slate-splitting demonstration (at the end of the tramway tour, but open to all). Tel. 0766/83 03 06.

Helpful Hints

The Welsh language is alive and well. In a pub, impress your friends (or make some) by toasting the guy who might have just bought your drink. Say "Yuchk-hid dah" (meaning "Good health to you") and "Dee och" ("Thank you"), or "Dee och on vowr" ("Thanks very much").

BLACKPOOL, ENGLAND'S CONEY ISLAND

Today you'll go from God's glorious garden to man's tacky, glittering city of fun, from pristine North Wales to the bells and blinkers of Blackpool. Blackpool, a middle-sized city with a six-mile beach promenade, is ignored by guidebooks (*Let's Go: Britain* in 570 pages of small print never even mentions Blackpool). Even the most thorough bus tour will show you castles till your ears crenellate but will never take an American visitor to Blackpool.

This is Britain's fun puddle, where every Englishman goes, but none will admit it. It's England's most visited attraction, the private domain of its working class. When I told Brits I was Blackpool-bound, their expression soured and they asked, "Oh God, why?" Because it's the affordable escape of North England's Ann and Andy Capps. It's an ears-pierced-while-you-wait, tipsy-toupee kind of place. Tacky, yes. Lowbrow, okay. But it's as English as can be, and that's what you're here for. The plan is to enjoy a slow morning in Ruthin, drive two hours, get set up, and spend the rest of the day just "muckin' about" (British for "messin' around"). If you're bored in Blackpool, you're just too classy.

Suggested Schedule	
9:00	Breakfast, slow morning.
10:00	Ruthin, free time, craft center, shopping.
11:00	Drive to Blackpool.
1:00	Arrive in Blackpool. Visit TI (follow signs) and set up in a B&B, buy show ticket, catch a trolley to the South Pier.
2:00	Pleasure Beach.
4:30	The Blackpool Tower.
7:30	Old Time Music Hall Show.
10:00	Prowl through the night lights, people, one-armed bandits, pubs, and clubs of England's Coney Island.

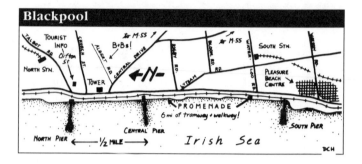

Transportation: Ruthin to Blackpool (100 mi.)

Blackpool's the hot spot, and on the motorways, you're a heat-seeking missile. From Ruthin, take A494 through the town of Mold and follow the blue signs to the motorway. M56 will zip you to M6, where you'll turn north toward Preston and Lancaster. After Preston, take M55 right into Blackpool and drive as close as you can to the stubby Eiffel-type tower in the town center. From here, you are a short walk away from the tourist office and the B&B district around Albert Road. Park carefully; petty vandals abound.

Sightseeing Highlights

Tourist Information Office—First of all, go to the helpful TI (tel. 0253/21623 or 21891 for 24-hour information). Get the city map (20p), pick up brochures from all the amusement centers, and go over your plans. Ask about special shows and evening events and seek advice on rooms. Remember, Blackpool is second only to London as a center for live theater.

▲**Blackpool Tower**—Much more than just a tower, this is a vertical fun center. You pay about £3 to get in, and after that the fun is free. Working your way up from the bottom, check out the fascinating aquarium, the bad house of silly horrors, the very elegant ballroom with barely live music and dancing all day, the room of discovery (funny mirrors and lots of hands-on curiosities—don't miss the "Meet Your Friends" chamber and the robot that verbalizes whatever you type). The finale is the tip of the tower. This symbol of Blackpool is a stubby version of its more famous Parisian cousin. The view from the top is smashing, especially at sunset. Consider a coffee break in the ballroom to watch the golden oldies dance to the grand pipe organ.

Survey Blackpool's six-mile beach promenade from a vintage trolley car. They go up and down the waterfront constantly, and it makes much more sense to ride them than to drive yourself. Gypsie Rosalee-type spiritualists are a fixture at Blackpool. I was told I mustn't leave without having my fortune told, but at £3 per palm, I'll read them myself.

▲▲Old-Time Music Hall Show—There are many shows at Blackpool, but its specialty is the old-fashioned variety show that went out with vaudeville. These are a great hit with "Twirlies" (senior citizens, infamous for using their bus passes "too early," before rush hour fades). The show is corny—neither hip nor polished—but it's fascinating to be surrounded by hundreds of partying British seniors, swooning again, waving their hankies to the predictable beat, and giggling at jokes I'd never tell my grandma. Busloads of happy widows come from all corners of North England to enjoy an "Old-Time Music Hall Show." Buy your ticket in the afternoon, about £3.50. Ask a local for the best show, probably on a pier.

The Illuminations—Every September and October, Blackpool stretches its season by "illuminating" its six miles of waterfront with countless lights all blinking and twinkling to the delight of those who visit this electronic festival. The American in me kept saying, "I've seen bigger and I've seen better," but I filled his mouth with cotton candy and just had some simple fun like everyone else on my specially decorated tram.

▲Pleasure Beach—These 42 acres of rides (more than 80, including "the best selection of white-knuckle rides in Europe"), ice skating shows, cabarets, and amusements attract six million people a year, making this England's most popular tourist attraction.

▲▲People Watching—Blackpool's top sight is its

people—old-timers strolling hand in hand. You'll see
England here like nowhere else. Grab someone's hand
and a big stick of "rock" (candy) and stroll.

Accommodations
Blackpool is in the business of accommodating people
who can't afford to go to Spain. Simple, inexpensive
B&Bs and hotels abound. The classy, expensive hotels
are, predictably, along the waterfront. Countless lackluster budget alternatives cluster, very handy and central,
around Albert Road, near the Central Pier and the tower.
These forgettable B&Bs almost all have the same
design—minimal character, maximum number of beds.
Double rooms (in the six or seven places I've visited) are
all the same small size, each with a small double bed,
your basic English breakfast, and a decent shower down
the hall. Prices range from £9 (dingy) to £14 (cheery) per
person. Arriving at midday, you should have no trouble
finding a place. September to November and summer
weekends are most crowded. I stayed at the **Belmont
Private Hotel** (inexpensive-moderate, 299 Promenade,
Blackpool South, FY1 6AL, tel. 0253/45815) right on the
waterfront, clean and friendly with good dinners and
view rooms. A less interesting but decent place is the
Pickwick Hotel, 93 Albert Road, Blackpool FY1 4PW,
tel. 0253/24229.

Itinerary Options
I'd skip Chester on this itinerary. It's a second-rate York,
but many people love old Chester, and you drive right by
it today. By leaving Ruthin at 9:00 a.m., you could have a
good two-hour look at Chester. If you'd like an especially
big dose of Coney Island, you could go direct to Blackpool and dive in.
    Liverpool, a gritty but surprisingly enjoyable city, is a
fascinating stop en route to Blackpool for Beatles fans
and those who would like to look urban England straight
in its problem plagued, not-a-fairy-tale-in-sight eyes.
(Tourist info.: tel. 051/709 36 31.) From Ruthin, get to the

M53, which tunnels under the Mersey River. Once in town, follow the signs to Pier Head and park just past the huge, curiously named Royal Liver Building in the Maritime Museum car park (£1.50 all day, safe, includes £1 admission to museum). The interesting Maritime Museum, cornerstone of a huge urban renewal project, tells the Liverpool story—ships, immigrations, hard times, and good times. Nearby are plenty of lively shops and restaurants. Beatles fans will want to explore Mathew Street a few blocks away, including the famous but boarded-up Cavern Club and the Beatles Shop at 31. "Beatle City" on nearby Seal Street is a museum chronicling the story of John, Paul, George, and Ringo. Another Liverpool attraction is its people. Be sure to break the conversational ice and get to know a Liverpudlian before you drive north along the waterfront following signs to M58, then M6, and finally M55 into the day's second pool—Blackpool.

Many people think I overrate Blackpool. If you're the kind of person who gets sick just thinking about rides, greasy spoon cafés, and cotton candy, skip or abbreviate Blackpool and head on to your Lake District home base.

THE WINDERMERE LAKE DISTRICT

Blackpool to the Cumbrian Lake District is another study in contrast. After a two-hour drive, you'll be in the heart of Wordsworth Country. If you never were a poet, here's your chance in a land where nature rules and man keeps a wide-eyed but low profile. Get oriented in the Lake District, enjoying a boat ride and the best six-mile walk it has to offer, before setting up in the most remote and scenic accommodations of the trip.

Suggested Schedule

9:00	Breakfast (earlier if possible—unlikely in Blackpool).
9:30	Drive north.
11:00	Visit Brockhole National Park Visitors Centre. See the orientation movie, then get a map and guide, talk to the information man, browse through exhibits, picnic on the grounds or lunch in the cafeteria.
1:00	Drive to Ullswater. Park at Glenridding.
1:45	Buy a boat ticket.
2:00	Catch the boat.
2:35	Hike from Howtown to Glenridding.
5:30	Drive to your B&B.

Transportation: Blackpool to Windermere (60 mi.)
Follow the M55 and M6 motorways north from Blackpool past Lancaster, exiting on A590, then to A591 through the towns of Kendal and Windermere to the Brockhole National Park Visitors Center, halfway between Windermere and Ambleside on A591 (allow two hours). From Brockhole, take the tiny road northeast directly to Troutbeck and then follow A592 to Glenridding and lovely Ullswater. Just before Glenridding, turn right into the car park and boat dock (40p self-service parking stickers). Catch the 2:00 boat, sail for 35 minutes, and walk for

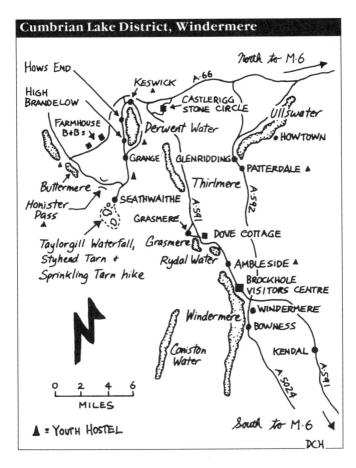

Cumbrian Lake District, Windermere

Hows End
High Brandelow
Farmhouse B+Bs
Keswick
North to M·6
A·66
Castlerigg Stone Circle
Derwent Water
Ullswater
Howtown
Grange
Glenridding
Patterdale ▲
Buttermere
Thirlmere
Honister Pass
Seathwaithe
Grasmere
Dove Cottage
Taylorgill Waterfall, Styhead Tarn + Sprinkling Tarn hike
Grasmere
Rydal Water
Ambleside ▲
Brockhole Visitors Centre
Windermere
Windermere
Bowness
Coniston Water
Kendal
A·591
A·592
A·5024
A·591
0   2   4   6
MILES
▲ = Youth Hostel
South to M·6
DCH

three hours back to the car. Then drive north along the lake, turning left on A5091 and left again on A66 to Keswick and your B&B over Newlands Pass.

Sightseeing Highlights
▲▲Brockhole National Park Visitors Centre—Start your visit to the Lake District here. Pick up a copy of "What's On at Brockhole." The center offers introduction-to-the-lakes slide shows daily at 11:00 a.m. and 2:30 p.m., an information desk, organized walks, special exhibits, a book shop, an excellent cafeteria, gardens, nature walks,

and a large car park. It is situated in a big, old, stately house on the shores of Windermere between Ambleside and the town of Windermere on A591 (open daily 10:00 a.m. to 6:00 p.m., £1.40 entrance fee, tel. 09662/6601). The important goal is to arrive here from Blackpool by 11:00 to catch the orientation show. Use the bookshop to buy the Ordnance Survey "Lake District Tourist Map" (£2.95) and a guidebook. I enjoyed the refreshingly opinionated *Good Guide to the Lakes* by Hunter Davies (£3.95). Go over your plans (Ullswater ferry schedule) with the information person.

The whole district is dotted with Tourist Information Centres. All are helpful, especially for their specific locality. Use them. Ask for advice. For the latest Lakes District weather report, call 09662/5151.

▲▲▲**Ullswater Hike and Boat Ride**—Ullswater is considered the most beautiful lake in the area, and this hike is a great way to enjoy it. Park your car at the Glenridding dock on the south end of the lake. Be sure to catch the 2:00 p.m. boat. (Boats leave Glenridding at 11:30 a.m., 2:00 p.m., and 4:30 p.m., sometimes more often. It's best to to get there 20 minutes early in summer; 35-minute ride; £1.70; tel. 08532/229 for information.) Ride to the first stop, Howtown, halfway up the lake. Then spend four hours hiking and dawdling along the well-marked path by the lake south about seven miles to Patterdale and then along the road back to your car in Glenridding. Good views, varied terrain, a few bridges and farms along the way. I did the walk in tennis shoes in three hours. Bring raingear. There are several steamer trips daily up and down Ullswater. A good rainy-day plan is to ride the boat up and down the nine-mile lake (two hours).

▲**Beatrix Potter's farm** (near Hawkshead next to Sawrey) gives a good look at her life and work, which is much more than children's books (daily except Thursday and Friday, 10:00 a.m. to 5:30 p.m.). For an easy walk, also near Hawkeshead, visit Tarn Hows.

Hard Knott Pass—Only 1,300 feet above sea level, this

pass is a thriller, with 1-in-3 gradients and a very narrow, winding road. Just over the pass are the scant but evocative remains of the Hard Knott Roman Fortress. Great views, miserable rainstorms.

Helvellyn—Often considered the best high mountain hike in Cumbria, this dangerous, thrilling four-hour hike from Glenridding has a glorious ridge-walk finale. Be careful, do this only in good weather, and get advice from the Glenridding tourist office. Stupendous views, but keep one eye on the trail.

Coniston Water Steamer Trip—for a pleasant 40-minute trip on a Victorian steam yacht, ride the *Gondola* (£3.00, from 11:00 a.m.).

Accommodations

The Lake District abounds with very attractive B&Bs, guest houses, and youth hostels. It needs all of them when summer hordes threaten the serenity of this romantics' mecca. The region is most crowded on Sundays and in July and August. Saturdays are not bad. With a car to shop around in, you should have no trouble finding a room, but for a particular place it's best to call ahead. The area's plentiful Tourist Information centers can give you B&B listings or book you a bed. Many phone numbers are due to change sometime soon, so use directory assistance if you have problems (0800-269-169).

Birkrigg Farm—This is the perfect farmhouse B&B for this trip. Mrs. Margaret Beaty serves visitors with a comfy lounge, evening tea (good for socializing with her other guests), classy breakfast, territorial view, perfect peace, and a hot water bottle to warm up your bed (farmhouses lack central heating). It's open late March through early November and Mrs. Beaty serves a fine £6 dinner for guests who order in advance (a good idea; only on Monday, Wednesday, and Friday). She'll pack a box lunch on request. Her 220-acre working farm is shown on the Ordnance Survey map, on the tiny road halfway between Braithwaite, near Keswick, and Buttermere (inexpensive, Birkrigg Farm, Newlands Pass Rd., Keswick, Cumbria,

CA125TS, tel. 0596/82-278 or, later, 07687/78278).
There's good food at the nearby Buttermere Inn.

Keskadale Farm B&B—Another great farmhouse
experience, valley views, flapjack hospitality, this is a
working farm with lots of curly-horned sheep (inexpensive with £5 dinners if booked in advance, open March
through November, on Newlands Pass Road near a hair-
pin turn. Call Mrs. Harryman at Braithwaite 544 or, later,
07687/78544).

For village B&Bs, try the beautiful Valley of Borrowdale
(south off Derwent Water). The village of Grange is nice,
but Rosthwaite is better. The **Yew Tree Farm** (tel.
059684/675 or, later, 07687/77675) and the **Nook Farm**
(Carole Jackson, tel. 059684/677 or, later, 07687/77677)
are each inexpensive and hearthocentric, with very old,
sagging floors, thick whitewashed walls, and small doorways. If you're interested in farm noises and the drafty
Old World, these are for you. But watch your head.

Ambleside—For a quiet, elegant splurge with a view
and great meals, stay at **Rowanfield Country Guest
House**, Kirkstone Road, Ambleside, Cumbria LA22 9ET,
tel. 05394/33686.

Youth Hostels—The Lake District has 30 youth
hostels and needs more. Most are in great old buildings,
handy sources of information, and fun socially. In the
summer, you'll need to call ahead. For this plan, consider
the **King George VI Memorial Hostel**—Good food,
royal setting, mile south of Buttermere Village on
Gonister Pass Road, tel. 059685/254 or, later, 07687/
70254; also, the **Lougthwaite Hostel**, secluded in Borrowdale Valley just south of Rosthwaite, well run, drying
rooms, tel. 059684/257 or, later, 07687/77257.
Two former hotels now operate as hostels: **Keswick** (tel.
72484) and **Derwentwater** (two miles south, tel.
059684/246). **The Patterdale hostel** (tel. 08532/394)
near Ullswater is very friendly. Remember, hostels are
marked on most good maps with a red triangle. **The
Westwater Youth Hostel** (tel.09406/222), on the
westernmost lake in the area, offers a romantic lakeside
setting . . . and bunk beds.

Itinerary Options

Consider seeing Wordsworth's Dove Cottage today rather than tomorrow. Skip the hike, do the Information Centre and Wordsworth's Dove Cottage. Or skip breakfast and do Brockhole Center 10:00 a.m. to 11:30 a.m., Dove Cottage 12:00 noon to 1:00 p.m., and then the hike. Or skip the Information Centre and do Dove Cottage. Visiting Wordsworth's place today makes tomorrow much easier.

If great scenery is commonplace in your life, the Lake District can be more soothing than exciting. To save time you could easily make this area a one-night stand—or even a quick drive-through.

EXPLORING THE LAKE DISTRICT

Fill today with your choice of great Lake District walks and a visit to the humble house of William Wordsworth, the poet whose appreciation of nature and back-to-basics life-style put this area on the map. If you need a vacation from your vacation, use this day to just vegetate and recharge.

Suggested Schedule

9:00	Slow breakfast, enjoy your farm.
10:00	Explore Buttermere Lake and drive over Honister Pass.
12:00	Lunch and drive to Grasmere.
1:00	Tour Wordsworth's Dove Cottage and museum.
3:00	Explore the lake called Derwent Water. See the town of Keswick, cruise to High Brandlehow Pier. Walk along lake to Hawesend Pier. Catch the boat back to Keswick.
6:00	Drive home (visiting Castlerigg Stone Circle if you have time and energy).

Transportation

Nothing is very far from Keswick and Derwent Water. The entire region is just 30 miles by 30 miles. By all means get a good map, get off the big roads, and leave the car, at least occasionally, for some walking. In the summer, the Keswick-Ambleside-Windermere-Bowness area suffers from congestion. Go west. Larger lakes are served by old "steamers," and any TI can give you local schedules.

Sightseeing Highlights

▲▲ **Dove Cottage**—Wordsworth spent his most productive years (1799-1808) in this well-preserved old cottage on the edge of Grasmere. Today, it is the obligatory sight for any visit to the area. Even if you're not a fan, Wordsworth's style of "plain living and high thinking," his appreciation of nature, and his basic romanticism are very appealing. The cottage tour is excellent as is the adjoining museum. Even a speedy, jaded museum-goer will want at least an hour here. (Open 9:30 a.m. to 5:30 p.m. April through September, Sunday from 11:00 a.m., and 10:00 a.m. to 4:30 p.m. off-season, £3).

Rydal Mount—Wordsworth's final, more high-class home, lovely garden, and view. It lacks the charm of Dove Cottage and is worthwhile only for Wordsworth fans.

▲▲**Derwent Water**—One of the region's most beautiful and most popular lakes. With five islands, a good circular boat service, plenty of trails, and the pleasant town of Keswick at its north end, the lake entertains. The roadside views aren't much, so walk or cruise. I suggest a combo hike/sail trip around the lake and an hour in Keswick (good shops and tourist information). The boats go every 15 minutes in each direction and make seven stops on each 50-minute round-trip. The best hour-long walk is between High Brandlehow and Hawesend. (There's a large car park at the Keswick pier and a small one above Hawesend.)

High Ridge Hike—For a great "king of the mountain" feeling, park your car at Hawesend, hike up along the ridge to Cat Bells, past the peak to Black Crag and down to High Brandlehow. From there take the easy path along the shore of Derwent Water back to your Hawesend starting point. Warning: Every year, careless hikers underestimate the need for good shoes, raingear, and maps. This lush world is not as gentle as it looks. Get specific hiking advice from a tourist center.

▲▲**A Waterfall and Two Tarns**—For a rewarding three-hour hike park your car south of Borrowdale at the end of a long dead-end road to Seathwaite. Go through the farm, cross the river, continue along the river (it's difficult to follow the trail; stay near the river) and up a steep, rocky climb to the Taylor Gill Force, a 140-foot waterfall. There's a tough hundred yards of rocky scramble, but the trail gets good at the falls. Keep walking to two lovely remote tarns (bodies of water too small to be lakes), circling the Seathwaite Fell to Stockley Bridge and following the bridle path back to your car. For an easy version, just hike to the first tarn and backtrack, eventually taking a right turn leading to Stockley Bridge (get advice at Keswick TI).

▲▲**Buttermere**—This is the ideal little lake with a lovely four-mile stroll around it offering nonstop lake land beauty. If you're not a hiker but kind of wish you were, take this walk. If you're very short on time, at least stop here and get your shoes dirty. A great road over the rugged Honister Pass connects Buttermere with Borrowdale and Derwent Water.

■▲**Castlerigg Stone Circle**—These 38 stones, 90 feet across, 3,000 years old, are, mysteriously, laid out on a line between the two tallest peaks on the horizon. Five minutes south of the A66, east of Keswick, well signposted from A66. Look for "stone circle" exit. For maximum goosebumps, be here at sunrise or sunset.

Sellafield Nuclear Power Plant—This leading British nuclear site had a reputation so bad it had to change its name. It now gives classy free tours to visitors (on the coast, just over Hard Knott Pass, tel. 09467/27027) and is an odd way to brighten up a gray day.

LAKE DISTRICT TO WEST COAST OF SCOTLAND

Today you drive for six hours to Oban, a gateway to the Hebrides, Scotland's wild and windblown western islands. The last half of the journey is scenic, taking you from big, burly Glasgow, along the famous Loch Lomond, deep into the powerful mountains, forests, valleys, and lochs of Scotland's west country and to the edge of the Highlands.

Suggested Schedule

9:00	Leave Lake District, stopping at the Castlerigg Stone Circle if you haven't yet. Drive for three hours to Glasgow.
1:00	Stop along Loch Lomond for picnic lunch. Drive on, three hours from Glasgow to Oban, enjoying the rugged scenery en route.
4:00	Arrive in Oban, go first to tourist office and then to your B&B.

Transportation: Lake District to Oban (220 mi.)
From Keswick, take A66 to M6 and speed nonstop north, crossing Hadrian's Wall into bonnie Scotland. Here the motorway ends, but the road (A74) stays great, becoming the M74 south of Glasgow. M74 becomes M8. Stay on M8 west through Glasgow. Take exit 17 and stay on A82. This throws you right onto A82 (in the direction of Dumbarton) to Loch Lomond. After Dumbarton, it's the A82, a beautiful lakeside drive along Loch Lomond.

Halfway up the loch, take a left onto A83, drive along saltwater Loch Long and toward Inveraray via Rest-and-be-thankful Pass. (This colorful name comes from the 1880s, when second- and third-class coach passengers got out and pushed the coach and first-class passengers up the hill!)

Inveraray is a lovely castle town on Loch Fyne. Leaving Inveraray, go through a gate (tricky to see) to A819,

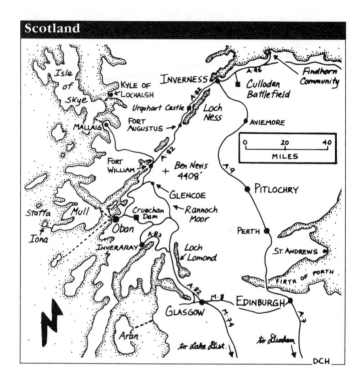

Scotland

DCH

through Glen Aray and along scenic Loch Awe where
you'll meet the A85. Turn left and follow this road into
Oban.

Oban

Oban is a nondescript but pleasant ferry terminal and
port town with a charming shiver-and-bustle vitality that
gives you a feel for small-town Scotland.

This "gateway to the isles" has ferries coming and
going all day long. The Isle of Mull (third largest in Scotland, very scenic, 300 miles of coastline, castle, 3,169-
foot-high mountain) is worth a day. Just beyond it, the
historic island of Iona (St. Columba brought Christianity
to this abbey in A.D. 590) can be visited easily as part of a
tour from Oban. I'd leave my car in Oban and take a tour.
Get specifics from the excellent TI (open Monday

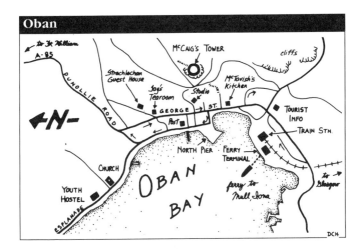

through Saturday 9:00 a.m. to 9:00 p.m., Sunday 10:00
a.m. to 5:00 p.m., shorter hours outside of July and
August, tel. 0631/63122). The stark but very green island
of Kerrera, just opposite Oban (six boats a day, 75p, from
Gallanach, two miles south of Oban), is a quick, easy
opportunity to get that romantic island experience. Enjoy
a walk, solitude, and the sea. The islands of Seil and
Luing, a short drive south, are another good side trip.
Staffa is a wondrous isle with natural caves, cliffs, and
columns.

  Oban itself has plenty going on in the summer. The TI
has handouts listing everything from saunas to laundromats to horse-riding to what to do in the rain. Use them.

Accommodations
Oban has plenty of B&Bs for its many visitors. The TI will
give you specifics and can find you a room if my sugges-
tions don't work.

  Strathlachlan Guest House—This is a winner. Mrs.
Rena Anderson's place is stocking-feet cozy, crackerjack
friendly, and chocolate-box tidy. There's a great lounge
and easy parking in a good central location two blocks
off the water just past Jay's Tearoom (inexpensive, 2
Strathaven Terrace, Oban, Argyll, tel. 0631/63861).

Achanmara Hotel—On the Esplanade waterfront promenade with an island view, three minutes from downtown, this is a grand old hotel with hotel-style formality (moderate, tel. 62683).

Rahoy Lodge—A bit eccentric, this "lived-in" lodge is on Gallanach Road about a mile south of town, overlooking the beach and islands (inexpensive, tel. 0631/62301).

Mrs. Robertson's B&B (moderate, Dungrianach, Pulpit Hill, Oban, Argyll, PA34 4LX, tel. 0631/62840) is a mini-estate overlooking the bay. Go up Albany Street, cross the railroad bridge, take the second right up Pulpit Hill, halfway up the road levels in woods, where you'll turn into the second driveway on the right. Look for a sign on a tree, before a telephone box. Also friendly, very cheap, popular with the *Let's Go* crowd, is **Jeremy Inglis B&B** (21 Airds Crescent, Oban, tel. 65065).

The **youth hostel**, on the Esplanade, alongside the finest hotels in town, is in a grand building with a grand piano, and a smashing harbor/island view (cheap, tel. 62025, open March through October only).

Food

Oban has plenty of eating options. In season, try to mix dinner and some Scottish folk entertainment. **McTavish's Kitchen** on central George Street is a plain-looking cafeteria that serves hearty, cheap food with live folk music and dancing most nights. **Jay's Tearoom** nearby is a comfy place with an interesting menu for a light meal.

The Studio on Craigard Road has a real hit-the-spot-on-a-stormy-day prawn-and-clam chowder. The **Oban Inn** is a fun local pub.

HIGHLANDS, LOCH NESS, SCENIC DRIVE

Today is mostly a scenic drive, your chance to see the harsh Highland beauty of Glencoe, the engineering beauty of the Caledonian Canal, and the soft beauty of Loch Ness—which is worth a look even if you don't believe in the monster. How far you get today depends on the weather, the traffic, and your eagerness to get to bonnie Edinburgh.

Suggested Schedule

9:00	Leave Oban.
10:00	Explore the valley of Glencoe, still weeping after the bloody clan massacre.
11:00	Drive from Glencoe to Fort Augustus.
12:00	Cut across Scotland, following the Caledonian Canal. Stop on Loch Ness to explore the castle, have a picnic, and take care of monster business.
3:00	Visit the evocative Culloden Battlefield, near Inverness.
4:00	Drive south.
7:00	Set up in Edinburgh.

Transportation: Oban to Glencoe (45 mi.) to Loch Ness (75 mi.) to Culloden and Inverness (20 mi.) to Edinburgh (150 mi.)

You'll make great time on good, mostly two-lane roads today unless traffic gets in the way. Americans are generally very timid about passing. Study the British. Be careful, but if you don't pass, diesel fumes and large trucks might be your memory of Day 16.

From Oban, follow the coastal A828, noticing the enchanting ruined island castle on your left a few minutes north of town. At Loch Leven and Ballachulish village, leave A828, go through the village on A82 into Glencoe. Drive into the valley for ten minutes until you hit the vast Rannoch Moor. Then make a U-turn and return through the valley. Continue north, over the bridge, past Fort William (helpful TI) and on toward Loch Ness. Scotland is sliced in half by a series of lakes and canals known as the Caledonian Canal. Follow the Caledonian Canal and A82 for 60 miles past Loch Ness to Inverness. Follow signs to A9 (south to Perth), and just as you leave Inverness (not worth a stop) turn east off A9 onto B9006 to the Culloden Battlefield Visitors Centre. Back on A9, it's a wonderfully speedy and very scenic highway (A9, M9, A8) all the way to Edinburgh. If traffic is light and your foot is heavy, you can drive from Inverness to Edinburgh in three hours. (For arrival in Edinburgh, see Transportation section, Day 17.)

Sightseeing Highlights

▲▲**Glencoe**—This is the essence of the wild, powerful, and stark beauty of the Highlands (and, I think, excuses the hurried tourist from needing to go north of Inverness). Along with its scenery, Glencoe offers a good dose of bloody clan history. Stop in at the visitors center to learn about the "murder under trust" of 1692, when the Campbells massacred the sleeping MacDonalds and the valley got its nickname, "The Weeping Glen."

Ben Nevis—At Fort William, you'll pass Ben Nevis, Great Britain's highest peak (more than 4,400 feet). Thousands of visitors walk to its summit each year, but just hope for a clear day and admire her from the car.

▲**Caledonian Canal**—Scotland is severed by three lochs (Oich, Lochy, and Ness) that were connected in the early 1800s by means of a series of canals and locks designed by the great British engineer, Telford. As you drive the 60 miles from Fort William to Inverness, follow Telford's work—40 miles of lakes, 20 miles of canals, and locks, raising ships from sea level to 51 feet (Ness) to 93 feet (Lochy) to 106 feet (Oich). For a good look at the locks, see "Neptune's Staircase" just after Fort William. Fort Augustus is the best stop. Drop into its free museum for more information.

▲**Loch Ness**—I'll admit, I had my eyes on the water. The local tourist industry thrives on the legend of the Loch

Ness monster. It's a thrilling thought, and there have been several seemingly reliable "sightings" (priests, policemen, and now sonar images). The Loch Ness Monster Information Centre (open 9:00 a.m. to 9:30 p.m. daily, £1.65, in Drumnadrochit) is tacky but the best way to satisfy your "Nessy" curiosity. The nearby Urquhart Castle ruins (Monday through Friday 9:30 a.m. to 7:00 p.m., Saturday and Sunday 2:00 p.m. to 7:00 p.m., £1) are gloriously situated with a view of virtually the entire Loch Ness and make for a better stop than the monster center. The Loch is deepest near this castle, and most sightings are in this area. Drumnadrochit has its Highland Games on the last Saturday of each August.

▲Culloden Battlefield—Bonnie Prince Charlie was defeated here in 1746. This last battle fought on British soil spelled the end of the Jacobite resistance and the fall of the clans. The visitors' center makes the short detour worthwhile with a great audiovisual show, a furnished old cottage, the memorial, and other exhibits. (Open daily 9:00 a.m. to 6:30 p.m., good tearoom, £1.50 entrance fee.)

Findhorn Foundation—This international spiritual community, famous for its sensitivity to nature and its tremendously green thumb, greets visitors with two tours a day on Monday, Wednesday, and Saturday. Findhorn is 20 miles east of Inverness; drive through Forres and follow signs to Findhorn. (The Park, Forres, Scotland IV36 0TZ, tel. 0309/30311.)

Pitlochry—This lovely mountain makes a pleasant overnight stop (TI open until 8:30, tel. 0796/2215, roomfinding service). Its Edradour Scotch distillery offers a fine guided tour, AV show, and of course, tasting (2 miles east of town, open daily 9:30 a.m. to 5:00 p.m., tel. 0796/2095). The Blair Athol Distillery (half a mile from the Tourist Office, tel. 2234) also gives daily free tours. Pitlochry also has a salmon ladder (April through October, free viewing area, ten-minute walk from town) and plenty of forest walks around the Tummel Forest Centre.

Scottish Words

aye—yes
ben—mountain
bonnie—beautiful
carn, cairn—heap of stones
creag, crag—rock, cliff
haggis—rich assortment of oats and sheep organs stuffed into a chunk of sheep intestine, liberally seasoned, boiled and eaten—mostly by tourists. Tastier than it sounds.
inch, innis—island
inver—river, mouth
kyle—strait, firth
loch—lake
neeps—turnips
tattie—potato

Accommodations

Here's where things get murky. You can get to Edinburgh if you really push. You'll arrive late, so be sure to have a firm hold on a bed and call at 5:00 p.m. with your estimated time of arrival (see Accommodations, Day 17). A more relaxed plan is to find a room somewhere between Culloden and Pitlochry. Inverness has plenty of rooms—but not much reason to stop. Good Inverness-area B&BS: **Woodside of Culloden** (inexpensive, in Westhill, just outside of town, tel. 0464/790242) and **Heathbank B&B** (inexpensive, south on A9 in Boat of Garten, Spey Ave. tel. 047983/234, fine haggis by Graham, nesting osprey nearby). I'd head south to find a place in the pleasant town of Pitlochry. Pitlochry's excellent **youth hostel** is on Knockard Road on a hill above the main street (£4.50, tel. 0796/2308). Also consider **Mrs. Maxwell's B&B** on Lower Oakfield Street (tel. 0796/2053).

EDINBURGH

Edinburgh is Scotland's showpiece. Historical, monumental, entertaining, well organized, it's a tourist's delight and, I think, one of Europe's great cities. You have nearly two days here—and you'll need every minute.

Suggested Schedule

9:00	Drive into Edinburgh from the Highlands.
12:00	Arrive in Edinburgh, park in central lot, do your TI chores, have lunch in the Waverley Center downstairs, or picnic in the Princes Street Gardens. Call your B&B to say you're in town. Browse through Waverley Center and the Princes Gardens.
2:00	Climb Scott Monument for an orientation view. Understand the town layout.
2:30	Georgian walk—down Rose Street, up Castle Street, left down George Street to Charlotte Square. Tour the Georgian House at 7.
5:00	Return to your car, drive to your B&B, and check in.

Option: If you arrived the night before, it would be best to visit the TI then or first thing this morning, and switch Days 17 and 18, doing the castle and Royal Mile first and the Georgian town with free time on the second day in Edinburgh.

Transportation

You'll be arriving the evening of Day 16 or about noon on Day 17, depending on which you favor—the country thrills of the Highlands or the city thrills of Edinburgh. Either way, follow the signs to "city centre" and the center's intersection of Princes Street and Waverley Bridge, under the black, towering neo-Gothic Scott Memorial. The best central car park is on New Street (over Waverley Bridge, left down to the end of Market Street, follow the blue "P" signs).

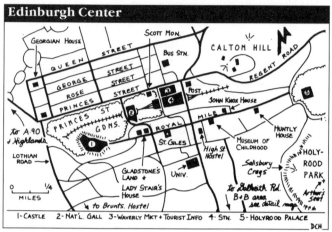

Edinburgh Center

1 - CASTLE   2 - NAT'L. GALL   3 - WAVERLY MKT + TOURIST INFO   4 - STN.   5 - HOLYROOD PALACE

Arriving in the Evening: Park wherever you can and run into the TI (open until 9:00 p.m. in July and August) before driving to your B&B. Call your B&B upon arrival to explain your plans (without the TI's help—they'll take a commission). To get to my B&B listings, go over the Royal Mile on Bridge Street and follow the green A68 signs (in the direction of Jedburgh). Take the first left after the huge Commonwealth Games swimming pool and sports center (on your left).

You won't need your car again until you leave Edinburgh. City buses (up-to-date routes listed in basic 20p city map at TI; average fare 40p) and taxis (easy to flag down, several handy pick-up points, 90p drop charge, average ride between downtown and the B&B district—£1.50) are easy and inexpensive, whereas parking and traffic are a real headache. Nearly all Edinburgh sights are within walking distance.

Orientation

Edinburgh is two towns divided by what was once a lake. The lake (Nor Loch) was drained and is now a lovely park and community center containing the helpful TI, Waverley Shopping Center, the train station, the starting point for most city bus tours, the festival office, the National Gallery, and a covered dance and music pavilion.

The old town grew along a volcanic ridge running south of the lake. Historic, fascinating buildings pack the Royal Mile bounded on the summit by the great castle and on the bottom by the Holyrood Palace. Houses, shops and arcades are tall and shoulder-to-shoulder, with "closes," or little courtyards, connected to High Street by narrow lanes or even tunnels. This colorful jumble, in its day the most crowded city in the world, is the tourist's Edinburgh.

To alleviate crowding, the lake was drained and a magnificent Georgian city, today's New Town, was laid out to the north. Georgian Edinburgh, like Bath, shines with broad boulevards, straight streets, square squares, circular circuses, and elegant mansions decked out in colonnades, pediments, and sphinxes in the proud, neoclassical style of 200 years ago.

Your first stop on arrival must be the TI located central as can be atop the Waverley Market on #3 Princes Street (open Monday through Saturday 8:30 a.m. to 9:00 p.m. and Sunday 11:00 a.m. to 9:00 p.m. in July and August; Monday through Saturday 8:30 a.m. to 8:00 p.m. and Sunday 11:00 a.m. to 8:00 p.m. in June and September; and Monday through Friday 9:00 a.m. to 6:00 p.m. and Saturday 9:00 a.m. to 1:00 p.m. in the off-season; tel. 031/557-2727).

Buy a city map (20p, with up-to-date bus routes) and pick up the "Welcome to Edinburgh" leaflet, *What's On*, and "Walking Tours in the City Center" brochures. ("Robin's Tours" are excellent, tel. 661-0125.) Confirm your sightseeing plans and hours as described below, and ask about walking tours down the Royal Mile, evening events and entertainment, and midday concerts in the park. The bank in the TI has long hours and fair rates.

Accommodations

Edinburgh, the festival city, is packed in the summer, but it has lots of B&Bs, hotels, and hostels and a super tourist office to make the needed arrangements.

The annual festival fills the city every year in the last half of August (August 11-31 in 1991). Conventions, school holidays, and other surprises can make room-finding tough at almost any time. Arrive early or telephone your B&B earlier in your trip. Use the TI (their room-finding service is expensive, it costs you £1 and your B&B 10 percent, so use it only as a last resort).

The best B&B district is, without a doubt, south of town. You'll find street after street of B&Bs south of the Royal Commonwealth Pool just off Dalkeith Road. This area is a 20-minute walk from the Royal Mile, well served by city buses, comfortably safe, and loaded with eateries, laundromats, shops, and so on.

Millfield Guest House—Mrs. Liz Broomfield's place is great, on a quiet street, around the corner from the bus stop, with easy parking and an entertaining proprietor. It's furnished with antique class, sit-and-chat ambience, and a comfy TV lounge (inexpensive-moderate, 12 Marchhall Rd., just east off Dalkeith Rd., south of the pool, tel. 031/667-4428).

Ravensneuk Guest House is also great (moderate, nearby at 11 Blacket Ave., across Dalkeith Rd., tel. 031/667-5347).

Thrum's Private Hotel—This small hotel offers rooms with private bathrooms (expensive, 14 Monto St., tel. 667-5545).

Allan Lodge Guest House—Delightful location on a quiet crescent between Dalkeith Road and Minto Street (inexpensive-moderate, including free access to a private park behind the house, 37 Queen's Crescent, tel. 668-2947).

Santa Lucia Guest House—Friendly accommodations run by effervescent Mrs. Laird, a great value (moderate, 14 Kilmaurs Terrace, tel. 667-8694).

Kenvie Guest House—Friendly, with lots of intimate, caring touches, run by Richard and Dorothy Vidler (inexpensive, 16 Kilmaurs Rd., EH165DA, tel. 668-1964).

Priestville B&B, run by Jim and Audrey Christie, is another comfy and friendly place (inexpensive, 10 Priestfield Rd., Edinburgh EH16 5HJ, tel. 031/6672435).

These B&Bs (and many more nearby) are well served by buses. On Dalkeith, 14, 21, 33, and 3C green buses take

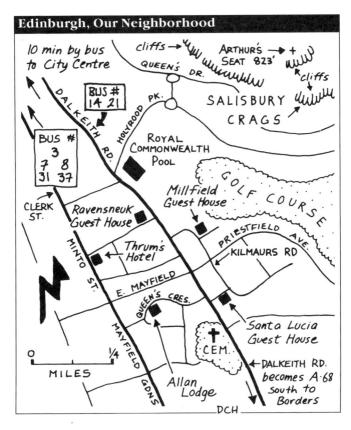

Edinburgh, Our Neighborhood

10 min by bus to City Centre

cliffs →

QUEEN'S DR.

ARTHUR'S → + SEAT 823'

↖cliffs

BUS # 14 21

HOLYROOD PK.

SALISBURY CRAGS ↗

DALKEITH RD.

BUS # 3 7 8 31 37

ROYAL COMMONWEALTH POOL

GOLF COURSE

CLERK ST.

Ravensneuk Guest House

Millfield Guest House

PRIESTFIELD AVE.

MINTO ST.

Thrums Hotel

←KILMAURS RD.

E. MAYFIELD

QUEEN'S CRES.

MAYFIELD GDNS.

Santa Lucia Guest House

0   ¼

MILES

+ CEM.

←DALKEITH RD. becomes A·68 South to Borders

Allan Lodge

DCH

you downtown. On Minto Street, 3, 7, 8, 31, and 37 do the same (routes may change; see the TI city map). The handy laundromat on 208 Dalkeith, open Monday through Friday 8:30 a.m. to 5:00 p.m., Saturday and Sunday 10:00 a.m. to 2:30 p.m., charges £2.30 for a self-serve load. Pay just 40p more, and they'll do it for you. The friendly manager can even drop your clean clothes back at the B&B for you. There's a wonderful take-out Chinese food on Minto Street and a handy cafeteria overlooking huge Commonwealth Pool.

Dorms and Hostels: Although Edinburgh's youth hostels are well run, open to all, and provide a £6 or £7 savings over B&Bs, they include no breakfast and are comparatively scruffy and dreary. They are **The Brunts-field Hostel** (on a park, 7 Bruntsfield Crescent, buses 11, 15, 16 to and from Princes St., tel. 447-2994), the **Edinburgh Hostel** (17 Eglinton Crescent, tel. 337-1120), the **High Street Independent Hostel** (young, hip, well run, huge rooms, scruffy, videos, my mom wouldn't sleep a wink here but my little sister would dig it, just off the Royal Mile, very central, at 8 Blackfriars St., tel. 557-3984), and **Cowgate Tourist Hotel** (student dorms, open for tourists early July through mid-September, very central, just off Royal Mile, bleak, basic, but full of good services, kitchen, laundry, double and single rooms only, £6 per person, 112 The Cowgate, tel. 031/2262153).

Patrick Geddes Hall—For the most central budget beds, consider this university dorm, open late June to late September, very basic twins and singles with breakfast right under the castle overlooking the National Gallery and city park. You'll find it exactly halfway between the castle and the train station, below Lawnmarket. Tel. 225-8400, £16 per person but only £10 "standby" price for those arriving after 6:00 p.m.

Food

Restaurants are good, plentiful, and varied in Edinburgh. Here are a few ideas that might fit your sightseeing plans, palate, and budget.

Light Meals along the Royal Mile: Historic pubs and doily cafés with reasonable, rather unremarkable meals abound. For a cheap lunch in legal surroundings, try the cafeteria in the **Parliament House** (entry behind St. Giles church near parking spot 21). Or munch prayerfully in the **Lower Aisle** restaurant under St. Giles church. Best picnic spot is in the hidden **Italian Gardens** down a quiet lane next to Clarinda's Tea Room near the bottom of the Royal Mile. This peaceful oasis is open to the public.

Eating in the New Town: Edinburgh seems to be a lunching kind of place. Local office workers pile into **Lanterna** for very good Italian food (family run, fresh

and friendly, ask about their lunch special, 83 Hanover
St., two blocks off Princes St., tel. 226-3090). Rose Street
has tons of pubs. The **Waverly Center Food Circus**
(below the TI) is a ring of flashy, trendy, fast-food joints
offering a plastic galaxy of choices. At Waverly, try
McTavishes for such hearty, inexpensive, and traditional
local specialties as haggis. The **Caravelle** serves good
three-course lunches and traditional Scottish high tea
(light, genteel meal, 5:00 p.m. to 7:00 p.m.). The lush city
park is ideal for picnicking.

   Dalkeith Road Area—Near Your B&B: The huge
Commonwealth Pool has a cafeteria for hungry swim-
mers and budget travelers (pass the entry without paying,
sit with a poolside view). For very good Scottish food, eat
at the **Golden Coin** (moderate-expensive, across the
street from the Commonwealth Pool). Just around the
corner from the pool (at 58 Dalkeith Rd., tel. 667-1816) is
the **Unco Guid** restaurant, serving tasty and traditional
Scottish meals at moderate prices. For great fish-and-
chips, **Brattesani** at 87 Newington Road (a block east of
the pool) is good. Don't order the milkshakes; if you need
some cheap haggis, they've got it. The **Chatterbox** (9:30
a.m. to 7:00 p.m., down Preston St. from the big pool) is
fine for a light meal. The nearby **Wine Glass Pub** is the
''in'' place for the local crowd, with great atmosphere.

   A ''Scottish Evening'' Dinner: There are plenty of
touristy Scottish Evenings in the city's ritzy hotels and
always a few scruffy pubs featuring local folk bands listed
at the tourist office.

   Just off the Royal Mile on Cockburn Street, the **Malt
and Shovel Pub** is a typical Edinburgh pub with the best
selection of malt whiskey in town.

EDINBURGH

Continue your look at Edinburgh, visiting the castle and exploring along your way down the history-packed Royal Mile to the Holyrood Palace. Your Scottish finale will be an evening of folk fun, food, and music.

Suggested Schedule

8:30	Breakfast, drop off laundry, and bus to High Street or taxi to Castle Esplanade.
9:30	Tour the castle.
11:00	Do the Royal Mile: Gladstone Land, Lady Stair's House, pub lunch, St. Giles Church, Knox's House, Huntly House, Craft Center.
4:00	Tour Holyrood Palace.
7:00	Scottish Evening—dinner show in hotel or simple dinner and folk music in a pub.

Sightseeing Highlights along the Royal Mile

▲▲▲ Royal Mile—This is one of Europe's most interesting historic walks, whether you follow a local guide (daily, free during the festival, £3 other times) or do-it-yourself with a Royal Mile guidebook. Each step of the way is entertaining. Start at the top and loiter your way downhill to the palace. Following are the top sights of the Royal Mile—working downhill.

All along this Royal Mile, which is actually a series of different streets in a straight line, you'll find interesting shops, cafés, and "closes" (public lanes branching off into peaceful little courtyards) providing the thoughtful visitor a few little rough edges of the old town, which in a few years will be a string of tourist gimmicks, woolen shops, and contrived "sights."

▲▲ Edinburgh Castle—The fortified birthplace of the city 1,300 years ago, this is the imposing symbol of Edinburgh. Start with the free 20-minute guided introduction tour, which starts every few minutes from inside the gate. (See the clock for the next tour.) Don't miss the Scottish

National War Memorial, the Banqueting Hall with fine Scottish Crown Jewels, the room full of Battle of Culloden mementos, St. Margaret's Chapel (oldest building in town), the giant cannon, and the city view from the ramparts (best seen in that order). Allow 90 minutes including the tour. You can enter the castle Monday through Saturday 9:30 a.m. to 4:20 p.m., Sunday 12:30 p.m. to 3:35 p.m. Costs £2.20.

▲▲**Gladstone's Land**—Take a good look at a typical sixteenth-century to seventeenth-century house, complete with lived-in furnished interior and guides in each room. The best Royal Mile photo is from the top floor window or from the top of its entry stairway through the golden eagle. Open April through October, Monday through Saturday 10:00 a.m. to 5:00 p.m., Sunday 2:00 p.m. to 5:00 p.m.

▲**Lady Stair's House**—This interesting house, which dates back to 1622, is filled with manuscripts and knick-knacks of Scotland's three greatest literary figures: Robert Burns, Sir Walter Scott, and Robert Louis Stevenson. Interesting for anyone, orgasmic for fans. Open 10:00 a.m. to 5:00 p.m., closed Sunday.

St. Giles Cathedral—Don't miss the ornate, medieval thistle chapel or the Scottish crown steeple in this engaging Gothic church. John Knox, founder of austere Scottish Presbyterianism, is buried, austerely, under the parking lot (spot 44).

The Parliament House—Stop in to see the grand hall with its fine hammerbeam ceiling and stained glass. For a trip into the eighteenth century, drop by Tuesday through Friday around 10:00 a.m or 10:30 a.m. to see all the wigged and robed legal beagles hard at work. You are welcome to observe any trials in action. The doorman is helpful (entry behind St. Giles Church near parking spot 21, open to the public daily).

John Knox's House—Fascinating for Reformation buffs. This fine sixteenth-century house is filled with things from the life of the Great Reformer. Monday through Saturday 10:00 a.m. to 5:00 p.m., firmly closed on Sunday, £1.

▲**Huntly House**—Another old house full of old stuff, it's free and worth a look for its early Edinburgh history. Don't miss the copy of the National Covenant written on an animal skin or the sketches of pre-Georgian Edinburgh with its lake still wet. Open 10:00 a.m. 5:00 p.m., closed Sunday.

Crafts Center in the Acheson House (in courtyard next to Huntly House)—This is Edinburgh's best, filled with the work of a local network of 300 craftspeople. Free.

▲**Holyrood Palace**—At the bottom end of the Royal Mile, this is where the queen stays when she's in town. Guided tours only of the royal apartments, state apartment, and lots of rich furnishings, paintings, and history. Open Monday through Saturday 9:30 a.m. to 5:00 p.m., Sunday 10:30 a.m. to 6:30 p.m. (often closed when in use, so ask at at the TI), £2.

The Brass Rubbing Centre—(Trinity Apse, Chambers Close, off the High Street near the bottom of the Royal Mile) is excellent if you've yet to rub a brass tombstone. And the **Museum of Childhood** offers a fine look at old toys (38 High St., Monday through Saturday 10:00 a.m. to 6:00 p.m., free).

Other Edinburgh Sightseeing Highlights

▲**Walter Scott Monument**—An elaborate, neo-Gothic monument (like Albert Memorial and Houses of Parliament in London) honoring the great author, one of Edinburgh's many illustrious sons. (Built in 1840, 200 feet high, 287 steps to a fine city orientation view.)

▲▲**Georgian Edinburgh**—The grand George Street connects St. Andrew and Charlotte squares. This is the centerpiece of the elegantly planned New Town. Don't miss the refurbished Georgian House at 7 Charlotte Square with its interesting video introduction and a lady, bursting with stories and trivia, in each lavish room. Open Monday through Saturday 10:00 a.m. to 5:00 p.m., Sunday 2:00 p.m to 5:00 p.m., shorter hours off-season. More fine examples of Georgian planning are Edinburgh's lovely squares beyond Charlotte Square: Moray Place (notice the plaques; this is where doctors do private surgery), Ainsley Place, and Randolph Crescent.

▲**Arthur's Seat**—A 30-minute hike up the 822-foot volcanic mountain (surrounded by a fine park overlooking Edinburgh), starting from the Holyrood Palace or the Commonwealth Pool, gives you a rewarding view. It's the easiest "I climbed a mountain" feeling I've ever had. You can drive most of the way up from behind. Follow the one-way street from the palace.

Princes Street Gardens—This grassy former lakebed separates Edinburgh's new and old towns with a wonderful escape from the citiness of it all. There are plenty of concerts and dances in the summer and the oldest floral clock in the world. Join local office workers in a picnic lunch break.

National Gallery—An elegant neoclassical building with a small but impressive collection of European masterpieces and the best look you'll get at Scottish paintings. (Monday through Saturday 10:00 a.m. to 5:00 p.m., Sunday 2:00 p.m. to 5:00 p.m., free.)

A Scenic Bus Ride—For a quick lift around town, take advantage of Edinburgh's bus service 99. It circles the town center—Royal Mile, Calton Hill and Princes Street—and for one cheap ticket you can stop and go all day. It's narrated, and on sunny days it goes topless.

Royal Commonwealth Games Swimming Pool—The biggest pool I've ever seen. Open to the public, swimsuit and towel rentals, good cafeteria, weights, saunas, and Europe's biggest flume (water slide).

City Bus Tours—Edinburgh offers a stunning array of tours taking you around the city or around Scotland. The half-day tours of greater Edinburgh take over where your feet leave off. One-day tours can take you as far as the Western Islands, Oban, and Loch Ness. Tours leave from the Mound, near the train station. "The Sea, the City and the Hills" is the best two-hour tour of greater Edinburgh (£2.50). You can book tours at the TI.

Greyhound Races—If you've never seen dog racing,

this is a fun night out combining great dog- and people-watching with a chance to lose some money gambling. Races are held about two nights a week at Powderhall Stadium (see "What's On" schedule).

Edinburgh Crystal—Blowing, molding, cutting, polishing, engraving, The Edinburgh Crystal Company gives a great glassworks tour (it smashes Venice). Drive ten miles south of town (on A701) to Penicuik. Forty-five-minute tours leave at regular intervals between 9:15 a.m. and 3:30 p.m., Monday through Friday (£1). There is a shop full of "bargain" second-quality pieces, a video show, and a good cafeteria. Consider half-day tours from the Mound or doing it tomorrow on your way south. Call first, (0968/75128); avoid the 12:00 to 1:00 factory lunch break.

Stirling Castle—It's popular but currently used as a barracks and nowhere near as interesting as Edinburgh's castle. The town is pleasantly medieval, however, and many commute (one hour by train) to the more hectic Edinburgh from here. (TI tel. 0786/75019.)

▲▲▲ **The Edinburgh Festival**—One of the events of Europe, the annual festival turns Edinburgh into a carnival of culture. There are enough music, dance, art, drama, and multicultural events to make even the most jaded tourist drool with excitement. Every day is jammed with formal and spontaneous fun. The festival rages from mid-August through September's first week (August 11-31 in 1991), with the Fringe Festival and the Military Tattoo starting a few days early. Many city sights run on extended hours, and those that normally close on Sundays don't. Local students give free Royal Mile walking tours. It's a glorious time to be in Edinburgh.

Although major events sell out well in advance, 10 to 15 percent of all tickets are held to be sold at 8:00 a.m. on the day of the show. Just line up at the show office at 21 Market Street (tel. 225-5756). Every day is packed with top-notch ticket-at-the-door opportunities for minor events. Look into tickets from London at the start of your tour and do whatever you can to get a ticket to the massed bands, drums, and bagpipes of the Military Tattoo (nightly except Sunday, August 2-24 in 1991, at the castle, tel. 225-1188 for information). Keep in mind that the more informal and equally wonderful Fringe Festival (information tel. 226-5259, bookings tel. 226-5257) has hundreds of events for which tickets are sold only at the door. Pick up the "Fringe Program" and the "Festival Times" for schedules and reviews. Your major festival worry is getting a room. After that, get a program, and you're a hyper kid in a cultural wading pool. If you do manage to hit the festival, be sure to add at least a third day here.

Shopping—The best shopping is along Princes Street (don't miss elegant old Jenner's Department Store), the mod and flashy Waverley Center, and the Royal Mile. (Shops are usually open from 9:00 a.m. to 5:30 p.m., later on Thursday.)

▲▲**Folk Music**—Edinburgh offers both folk music in pubs and more organized "Scottish folk evenings," generally in more expensive hotels. For £20 to £25 at several hotels on nearly any night you can enjoy a traditional— or at least what the tourists believe is traditional—meal with the full slate of swirling kilts, blaring bagpipes, and colorful Scottish folk dancing. You can get plenty of specifics at the TI or in *What's On*. For a basic informal evening of folk music, find the right pub. My favorite Scottish band, the North Sea Gas, plays every Friday, 8:30 p.m. to 11:00 p.m., free, at Platform One in the Caledonian Hotel on Princes Street. Pubs that regularly feature folk music are the White Hart (Grassmarket), Fables (West Port), Royal Oak (Infirmary St.), and the Waverley Bar (St. Mary St.). Preservation Hall (Victoria Street) is good for jazz and rock. *What's On* lists current folk music spots, and nearly any cabbie knows a hot spot or can find one by asking on his radio. (In general, cabbies are a great ace-in-the-hole source of information.) The Edinburgh Folk Club (tel. 229-6583) is a good bet for traditional music and dancing.

EDINBURGH—HADRIAN'S WALL—DURHAM

Head south from Edinburgh, filling today with fascinating sights A.D. 100, 1200, and 1900. We visit Hadrian's Wall, ancient Rome's northernmost boundary, marvel at Durham Cathedral, England's greatest Norman building, and relive the dawn of the twentieth century at the Beamish Folk Museum.

Suggested Schedule

8:30	Leave Edinburgh.
11:00	Arrive at Hadrian's Wall, tour the fort and Roman museum, take a walk along wall, lunch.
1:00	Drive to Beamish Museum.
2:00	Beamish Open-Air Museum.
5:00	Drive to Durham.
5:30	Arrive Durham, visit TI, get B&B, tour cathedral.

Transportation: Edinburgh to Hadrian's Wall (100 mi.) to Beamish (40 mi.) to Durham (10 mi.) to York
From Edinburgh, Dalkeith Road leads south, becoming A68. (There's a handy supermarket on the left just as you leave Dalkeith Town, ten minutes south of Edinburgh, parking behind). A68 takes you all the way to Hadrian's Wall in 2 hours. You'll pass Jedburgh and its abbey after one hour. (There's a coach tour's delight just before Jedburgh with kilt makers, woolens, and a sheepskin shop. In Jedburgh, across from a lovely abbey, is a free parking lot, a good visitor's center, and public toilets.) The England/Scotland border (great view and Mr. Softy ice cream and tea caravan) is a fun quick stop. Before Hexham, roller-coaster down A6079 two miles to B6318. This great little road follows the Roman wall westward. Notice the wall and its trenches on either side. After ten minutes and several "severe dips" (if there's a certified nerd or bozo in

Edinburgh-Hadrian's Wall-Durham

EDINBURGH

JEDBURGH

HOLY ISLAND

NEWCASTLE

BORDERS

BEAMISH FOLK MUS.

MIDDLESBROUGH

STAITHES

WHITBY

HADRIAN'S WALL

DURHAM

DANBY

NORTH YORK MOORS

HUTTON-LE HOLE

YORK

to Cambridge via A·1 & M1

0 — 50 MILES

DCH

the car, these road signs add a lot to a photo portrait), pull into the Housestead's Roman Fort information center. The Roman fort is on the right.

After your visit, take the small road past Vindolanda (another Roman fort and museum) to the A69. Go east past Hexham, then south on the A68. After a few miles, turn east on B6278 through lovely little Snods Edge and through Blackhill to Stanley. The Beamish Museum is well signposted between Stanley and Chester-le-Street.

If you're taking the A1 from Edinburgh south to Beamish, be sure to avoid Newcastle by taking the Tyne River Tunnel. Beamish is clearly signposted from the M1, which starts just after the tunnel. Durham is eight miles south of Beamish.

After the museum, follow the signs west past Chester to the Motorway. Head south. Just before you enter Durham's old town center (cathedral and castle), turn left into the modern high-rise parking lot. Parking in old Durham is miserable. From the seventh floor, a walkway takes you right into the old town. The route from Durham south to the North York moors is tricky. Whatever you do, don't get sucked into the Stockton-Middlesbrough mess. Take the motorway all the way to Darlington before heading east.

Sightseeing Highlights

▲▲▲ **Hadrian's Wall**—One of England's most thought-provoking sights. The Romans built this great stone wall during the reign of the emperor Hadrian (around A.D. 130) to protect England from invading Scottish tribes. It stretches 74 miles from coast to coast. Defended by nearly 20,000 troops, with castles every mile, it was flanked by ditches, 15 feet high and wide enough to allow chariots to race from mile castle to mile castle. Today, several chunks of the wall, ruined forts, and museums attract visitors.

By far the best single stop is the Housesteads Fort with its fine museum, national park information center (open daily 10:00 a.m. to 6:00 p.m., with car park and snack bar, tel. 049/363), and the best-preserved segment of the wall surrounded by powerful scenery. From Housesteads, hike west along the wall. Vindolanda, a larger Roman fort and museum, is just south of the wall and worth a visit only if you've devoured the Housesteads museum and are still hungry (tel. 04984/277).

For a good three-mile walk, go from Steel Rig (little road up from the Twice Brewed Pub) east along the crag and wall, past the mile castle sitting in a nick in the crag (39, called Castle Nick), to Housesteads.

The Twice Brewed Pub, 2 miles west of Housesteads, serves a good cheap bar lunch. The bartender can give you three possible explanations for the odd name of his place. If this place isn't cooking, there's another pub just east of there.

▲▲ **Beamish Open-Air Museum**—This huge, unique center energetically takes its visitors back to turn-of-the-century Northumbria. You'll need at least two hours to explore the 1900 town, train station, mining camp, and working farm. This isn't wax; it's real. Attendants at each stop explain everything, and an old tramway saves wear and tear on your feet (open 10:00 a.m. to 6:00 p.m., tel. 0207/231811, £4). The only museum I've seen covering the dawn of our century, Beamish was recently voted "European museum of the year."

▲▲**Durham Cathedral**—This is the best, least altered Norman cathedral in England and the only one in this itinerary. Study the difference between this heavy Romanesque ("Norman" is British for Romanesque) fortress of worship and the light-filled Gothic of later centuries (like York's Minster, tomorrow). Pick up the 10p guide, climb the 300 steps, and pay the 50 pence for a great view from the tower. There's also a good cafeteria. (Open 7:15 a.m. to 8:00 p.m. daily, until 5:00 p.m. September through May; 5:15 p.m. evensong services.)

The old town of Durham, surrounded on three sides by its river, cuddles the cathedral. It has a medieval cobbled atmosphere and an enjoyable market just off the main square but is exciting mostly for its cathedral.

Option: Holy Island and Bamburgh—Leaving Edinburgh, go around Arthur's Seat Park; at Holyrood Palace you'll pick up the A1. Follow the signs along the coast. After 50 miles of A1, take the small road to the Holy Island of Lindesfarne Gospels fame. Twelve hundred years ago this was Christianity's toehold on England. It's a pleasant visit, a quiet town with an evocative priory and striking castle, reached by a two-mile causeway that is cut off by high tides daily. Tidal charts are posted warning you when the place will become an island and you will become stranded (for tide information, tel. 0289/307283). For a very peaceful overnight, consider the Holy Island. A few good B&Bs cluster in the town center (tel. 0289/89218). A few miles farther down the coast is the grand Bamburgh Castle overseeing the most lovely stretch of beach in Britain. Its impressive interior is worth touring (open daily April through October from 1:00 p.m.).

Accommodations and Food—It's Your Option
Overnight in Durham: This is the easiest plan, stopping early and not having to rush Day 19. You'll be cutting the North York moors short to spend the evening in
the pleasant medieval city of Durham. Call ahead or visit
the TI on arrival, before visiting the cathedral. (TI open
Monday through Friday 9:00 a.m. to 6:00 p.m., Saturday
9:00 a.m. to 5:00 p.m., Sunday 2:00 p.m. to 5:00 p.m., tel.
091/384-3720, often posts B&B vacancies on its door
after hours.)

Most B&Bs are clustered west of the town center on
Crossgate and on Claypath. Because Durham is a historical area, B&B signs aren't allowed in yards or windows.
Your best bet is to ask at a neighborhood pub. Friendly
Robin and Freda Mellanby run the modern **Colebrick
B&B** (moderate, 21 Crossgate, Durham DH1 4PS, tel.
091/384-9585) with great castle and cathedral views and
easy parking, just a quarter mile from the town center.
The Victoria Pub (inexpensive, Hallgarth St., tel.
386-5269) offers B&Bs with fine old Victorian atmosphere. The **Durham Castle** is a student residence with
an elegant dining hall that serves meals and rents its 100
singles and 30 doubles to travelers from mid-July through
September (inexpensive-moderate, parking on cathedral
green provided, tel. 091/374-3850 or 374-3865). A fine
B&B is Mike and Anne Williams's **Castleview Guest
House** (moderate, 4 Crossgate, just over the Framwelgate
bridge near the town square, tel. 386-8852).

For dinner, the **House of Andrews** (at 73 Saddler St.
in the old town) and the **Almshouse** on the Palace Green
(open until 8:00 p.m.) are both good. There are lots of
inexpensive, spicy ethnic places. Most pubs serve no evening meals. The **Duke of Wellington**, about 1½ miles
out of town, is a great pub restaurant for a reasonable
dinner.

Staithes: Captain Cook's boyhood town, this is a salty
tumble of cottages bunny-hopping down a ravine into a
tiny harbor. Fishermen still outnumber tourists in undiscovered Staithes. The **Harborside Guest House**, right

on the waterfront, provides a basic bed, good meals (try the lobster), and the sound of waves to lull you to sleep (moderate, tel. 0947/840577).

If the guest house is full, you can try one of Staithes' several B&Bs. **Kirkhill House**, on Church Street up from Cook's house, has fine, inexpensive rooms. Call Rose Estill at 841058.

Getting to Staithes is no picnic. You'll have to brave the messy Middlesbrough motorway maze and head south on A173 toward Whitby until you see a sign for Staithes on your left. Whitby is a fun resort town with a busy harbor, steep and salty old streets, and a carousel of Coney Island-type amusements. Lots of B&Bs, a great abbey (with a good youth hostel next door; tel. 0947/602878), and a colorful people scene. Visiting here will rush your day, but if you want a mini-Blackpool, go for it (TI tel. 0747/602674). Like Staithes, it's just a short ride from the Moors.

On the north edge of the North York moors: To get an early start in the moors, leave Durham by 6:00 p.m. and find a place to sleep in the vicinity of Guisborough, Danby, and Goathland. You'll find plenty of good B&Bs in the romantic moors.

NORTH YORK MOORS AND YORK

Drive through the harsh heart of the North York moors for a good dose of its special stark beauty. Then set up and orient yourself in York, one of England's most exciting cities.

Suggested Schedule

8:30	Leave your Durham B&B at 8:00 (or 9:30 if you're already in moor country).
10:00	Danby Lodge—North York Moors Visitors Centre. Tour exhibit, pick up map, get help with moors plan.
11:00	Drive over the moors, taking a short stop at Hutton-le-Hole.
12:00	Drive to York.
1:00	Arrive at York, check into your B&B, park car for good, visit TI, lunch in King's Manor.
2:15	Walking tour of the city (at 7:00 p.m. in summer).
4:30	Railroad Museum or free in old town.

Transportation: Durham to Danby (75 mi.) to York (50 mi.)

Drivers will want to skirt the Middlesbrough snarls by taking motorway A1 south from Durham just past Darlington, to the A66 exit. From here, follow the little roads (A167, B1264, A1044, A171) east, toward Whitby. From Danby, explore through the North York moors south to Hutton-le-Hole and Pickering. From there, take A169 and A64 directly into York.

Sightseeing Highlights

▲**Danby Lodge**—This home of the North York Moors Visitors Centre is ideal for your moors orientation. It's a grand old lodge offering exhibits, special shows, and nature walks, an information desk with plenty of books and maps, brass rubbing, a cheery cafeteria, and bro-

chures on several good walks that start right there. Open
daily 10:00 a.m. to 5:00 p.m.

North Yorkshire Moors Railway—If you're tired of
driving (or without wheels), this 18-mile, 50-minute
steam engine ride from Grosmont and Goathland to Pickering goes through some of the best parts of the moors
almost hourly. Unfortunately, the windows are small and
dirty, and the tracks are in a scenic gully. (For information, tel. 0751/72508. For taped schedule information,
tel. 73535.) Pickering, with its rural life museum, castle,
and Monday market, is worth a stopover.

▲**Hutton-le-Hole**—This postcard-pretty town is home
of the fine little Ryedale Museum, which illustrates "farm-
life in the moors" through reconstructed and furnished
eighteenth-century local buildings. Car park and the public toilets are nearby (open daily 11:00 a.m. to 6:00 p.m.,
April through October).

Castle Howard—Especially popular since the filming of
Brideshead Revisited, this is a fine palatial home but
about half as interesting as Blenheim. Open late March
through October.

Rievaulx Abbey—A highlight of the North York moors
but a rerun of fine old abbeys you've already seen.

James Herriot fans—Pick up the brochure, "The Herriot Trail, a Circular Drive from Richmond in Wensley-
dale, Swaledale and Arkengarthdale." This is a good
optional side trip from Helmsley, Richmond, or York.

York

York is a walker's delight but a driver's purgatory. Don't
even think of taking the car through the old city gates.
Park near Bootham Road (actually just called Bootham).
All sights are within walking distance, and if you like, you
can pay £1.70 for an all-day pass on the yellow bus circuit
that goes around and around constantly, connecting the
major sights (with commentary; pick up flier at the TI).

The TI should be your first stop. Walk here after parking near Bootham. There's a good "long-stay" parking lot
just off Bootham; you'll see the big blue "P." If it's full,
look for other "P" signs on the map.

At the TI, pick up the mini-guide and map (30p, essen-
tial) and *What's On*. Consider the glossy official guidebook (£1.50, includes map), ask about special events, and
confirm your sightseeing plans (open Monday through
Saturday 9:00 a.m. to 8:00 p.m., Sunday 2:00 p.m. to 5:00
p.m.; October through May, Monday through Saturday
9:00 a.m. to 5:00 p.m., closed Sunday; tel. 0904/621756).

Accommodations

York has even more beds than tourists, and since you'll be
arriving around midday, finding a room should be fairly
easy. August (especially the last weekend) and Easter are the
most difficult times. The tourist office can find you a
room for a couple of dollars fee.

The handiest B&B neighborhood is Bootham, a five-
or ten-minute walk from the Minster, train station, and
TI. The side streets off Bootham are quiet, residential,
and freckled with B&Bs. Each place listed is small and
friendly, will hold a room with a phone call, and can
direct you to a nearby alternative if they're full. All are
helpful resources for sightseeing and eating in York.

The Bootham area has some easy streetside parking
and the St. Mary's long-term car park nearby, the handy
coin-op Clifton Laundrette (bring fifteen 10p coins and
four 20p coins for wash, soap, and dry), and several pubs
that serve evening meals. Here are my favorites:

Airden House—Snug and traditional, operated by
Susan and Keith Burrows, Airden House boasts a fine
lounge, some private parking, brightness and warmth
throughout (moderate, 1 St. Mary's, York Y03 7DD, tel.
0904/638915).

St. Mary's Hotel—These more hotelesque accommodations than the others are run by Cynthia Lister (moderate, 17 Longfield Terrace, tel. 626972).

Astoria Hotel—Mr. and Mrs. Bradley offer a good
value B&B (moderate, 6 Grosvenor Terrace, Bootham,
York, Y03 7AG, tel. 0904/659 558).

Bootham Bar Hotel—This small hotel is an eighteenth-
century building just within the city wall, only a scone's

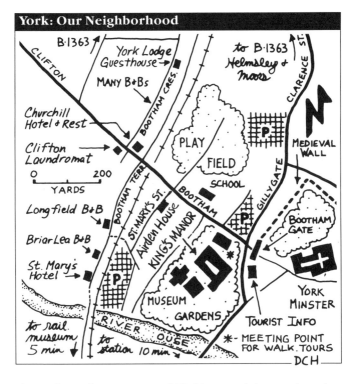

York: Our Neighborhood

B·1363 — CLIFTON

York Lodge Guesthouse →

MANY B&Bs

to B·1363 Helmsley & moors

CLARENCE ST.

Churchill Hotel & Rest

Clifton Laundromat

0 — 200 YARDS

BOOTHAM CRES.

BOOTHAM TERR.

PLAY FIELD

SCHOOL

P

MEDIEVAL WALL

GILLYGATE

Longfield B&B

BriarLea B&B

St. Mary's Hotel →

ST. MARY'S ST.

Arden House

KING'S MANOR

BOOTHAM

P

BOOTHAM GATE

P

MUSEUM GARDENS

TOURIST INFO

YORK MINSTER

RIVER OUSE

to rail museum 5 min ↓

to station 10 min ↘

* - MEETING POINT FOR WALK TOURS

DCH

throw from the Minster and TI. Not much better than the B&Bs but ideal locale. (Moderate-expensive en suite, 4 High Petergate, York YO1 2EH, tel. 658516.)

The Golden Fleece—For a funky, murky, creaky splurge right in the center of the old town, consider this historic 400-year-old pub. The floors aren't level, the beds are four-posters, and the local crowd fills the ground-floor pub with smoke and belly laughs (moderate, 16 Pavement, York, YO1 2ND, tel. 625171, private car park).

Youth Hostels—York has two fine central dorm-style budget alternatives to B&Bs. Both are just a few minutes' walk from the station and TI, require no membership, rent sheets, have no curfews, have pleasant TV lounges, and welcome travelers of all ages. The best is the **Youth Hotel** (£6 in twins, £4 in dorms, 11 Bishophill Senior Road, York YO1 1EF, tel. 625904 or 630613). It's clean, cheery, well run, with lots of extras like a kitchen, laundromat, games, and bar. They take no telephone reservations but normally have beds until noon. The **International House Hostel** is a bit depressing and musty, but you can't beat its price or location (£5 in four to six-bed rooms, one block in front of the TI at 33 Bootham, tel. 622874). One mile from the TI in the quiet town of Clifton is the official **IYHF hostel** (£6, tel. 65 31 47).

Food

For a cheap, historic, handy lunch near the TI, try the **King's Manor** on Exhibition Square (through the courtyard on the left, lunch only, Monday through Friday 12:00 noon to 2:00 p.m.).

Near the recommended B&Bs, **Elliot's Hotel Restaurant and Pub** serves good, inexpensive pub dinners (just off Bootham Terrace near the Longfield B&B, see map). Or go with the pub grub advice of the people who run your B&B.

For good meals downtown, consider **Bon Appetit** (10 St. Sampson's Square, tel. 627793, English and Continental food, good three-course £4 special before 7:00 p.m.), **Kites** (Grape Lane, fresh, unusual French and English meals moderately priced, around £6), and **Corallo's Pizza** (on Micklegate) for great pizzas in a pleasant atmosphere.

The **York Pie Shop** (moderate, on Pavement Street; 200 yards around the corner from the Jorvik Viking Center) is a café-type restaurant, doing traditional and "exotic" meat pies, salads, and daily specials.

Your best approach to eating in the constantly changing city of York is to follow local advice or wander around and eat at a place that looks good to you.

YORK

On this very busy York day, you start with a good look at its great church, wander through its wonderfully preserved medieval quarter, and spend the last half of the day immersed in the past—first reliving the 1800s in the Castle Museum and then going all the way back to the year 990 to visit the town the Vikings called Jorvik.

Suggested Schedule

9:00	Tour York Minster.
10:00	Browse through the old town and the Shambles.
1:00	York Castle Museum.
5:00	Jorvik Viking Center.

Sightseeing Highlights

▲▲**Walking Tours**—Volunteer local guides give free two-hour walks through York daily at 10:15 a.m. and 2:15 p.m. from April through October (plus at 7:00 p.m. from June through August). These tours, an ideal orientation, meet next to Bootham Bar across from the TI in Exhibition Square.

There are many other York walking tours. The popular ghost tours, offered after nightfall, and are the best of their kind in England.

▲**City Walls**—The historic walls of York provide a fine 2-mile walk. Be sure to walk from Bootham Bar (gate) to Monk Bar for outstanding cathedral views. Open until dusk; free.

▲**Railroad Museum**—This huge national museum shows 150 fascinating years of British railroad history. You'll see two roundhouses of historic cars and engines including Queen Victoria's lavish royal car, the very first "stagecoaches on rails," plus video shows and more. I think this is the best railroad museum anywhere. It's very popular, a ten-minute walk from the city center (open

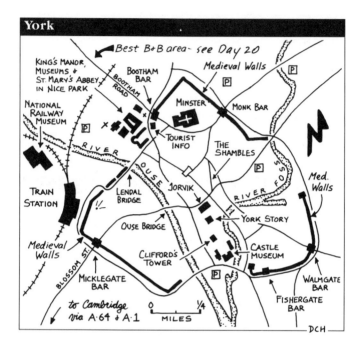

Monday through Saturday 10:00 a.m. to 6:00 p.m., Sunday 11:00 a.m. to 6:00 p.m.; £3, tel. 62 12 61).

▲▲▲The York Minster (cathedral)—The pride of York, this largest Gothic church in Britain is thrilling. Pick up the "Welcome to the York Minster" flier and ask at the information desk for a guided tour (or find someone with the Minster Guide armband)—fascinating and available almost on command. Highlights are the fine medieval stained glass, the undercroft showing foundations of Roman and Saxon buildings, the modern concrete save-the-church foundations, the treasure, and a moving display about the tragic 1984 fire and the worldwide support for the restoration work. Open daily from 7:00 a.m. to 8:30 p.m. Evensong daily at 5:00 p.m. but often without the "song." (Tour information tel. 624426.)

▲ The Shambles—This is the most colorful old York street and the half-timbered core of town. This area, between the core and the Minster and Monk Bar, is a window-shopper's delight.

▲▲▲**York Castle Museum**—Truly one of Europe's top museums, this is a walk with Dickens, the closest thing to a time-tunnel experience England has to offer. It includes a magnificent collection of old shops well stocked exactly as they were 150 years ago, costumes, armor, and the "every home needs one" exhibit showing the evolution of vacuum cleaners, toilets, TVs, bicycles, stoves, and so on, from their crude beginnings to now. Cafeteria, shop, car park (open daily 9:30 a.m. to 5:30 p.m., Sunday 10:00 a.m. to 5:30 p.m., £3, tel. 653611).

▲▲**Jorvik**—The innovative museum of Viking York takes you back 1,000 years—literally backward—in a little Disney-type train car. Then, still seated, you cruise slowly through the sounds, sights, and even smells of the re-created Viking village of Jorvik. Next you tour the actual excavation sight (best Viking dig I've seen anywhere) and finally get off to browse through a gallery of Viking shoes, combs, locks, and other intimate glimpses of their culture. Located on Coppergate, open daily 9:00 a.m. to 7:00 p.m., November through March 9:00 a.m. to 5:00 p.m., tel. 643211, £4. Don't be pressured into buying the colorful guidebook with your ticket. To minimize time in line—which can be more than an hour—go very early (at 8:45 a.m.) or very late (last entrance in summer is 7:00 p.m.). Crowds are worst from late July to mid-September and during school holidays. Some love this "ride", others call it a gimmicky rip-off. I like it.

DAY 22
YORK—CAMBRIDGE—LONDON

On this final day, you'll drive to Cambridge and probably turn in your rental car. Tour this historic town with its famous universities and lovely river. After dinner, take a quick train ride back to London, where you complete your circle of Britain by returning to your hotel of three weeks ago.

Suggested Schedule

9:00	Leave York, drive 150 miles south to Cambridge.
12:00	Arrive in Cambridge, leave your bags at train station, turn in your car, book a walking tour at the TI, have lunch.
2:00	Walking tour.
4:15	Free to explore, stroll through the Backs, shop in the center, go punting, or take a quick look at the Fitzwilliam Museum paintings.
7:04, 7:10, 7:22	Catch the 70-minute train ride to London's Liverpool Street or Kings Cross station (confirm these times at the station). Tube or taxi to your London hotel. Tour over. Everybody off the bus!

Transportation: York to Cambridge (150 mi.) to London (50 mi.)

Cambridge is a four-hour drive from York. York is such a mess, you'll want to ask at your B&B for the best way to get to A19 south to Selby. At Selby, cut west on A63 to A1 and follow A1 all the way south to Cambridge. There is a tempting motorway (M1) farther west, but stick to the A1, which is near-motorway quality and a more interesting drive. (Romantics will be tempted to visit Sherwood Forest, where Robin Hood and his Merry Men practiced Reaganomics in reverse so long ago. The Sherwood Forest visitors center, ten minutes south, off the A1 near

Edwinstowe north of Nottingham, doees its best to resurrect the legend with an exhibit, cafeteria, and "historical" walks in the nearby woods.) Finally, come into Cambridge on the A604, following the signs to the town center. Park as centrally as you can. Driving in Cambridge is somewhere between a headache and impossible. The huge, central Lyon Short Stay Parking Lot is handy.

Cambridge to London: From Cambridge, if you're driving to London, any major road going west or south will direct you to the M11 motorway. It's 60 high-speed miles (with no gas stations) to the London ring road. Needless to say, driving in London is no fun. Be sure to catch the poorly marked M25 outer ring road (you'll see Heathrow and Gatwick signs) and circle around to the best position to start your central attack. (You can buy a good London map at the Cambridge TI for 50p.) If you do decide to drive into London—where your car is a useless headache—you'll learn why I recommend . . .

Leaving Your Car in Cambridge: Ideally, you picked up a car at Heathrow that can be dropped at Cambridge. Hertz (Willhire Limited, 41 High St., Chesterton, tel. 68888), Budget (303 Newmarket Rd., tel. 323838), Kenning (47 Coldhams Lane, tel. 61538), Avis (243 Mill Rd., tel. 212551), and Godfrey Davis/EuropCar (315 Mill Rd., tel. 248198)—all the major rental agencies allow you to pick up in Heathrow and drop in Cambridge. With this plan, you'll drive to the Cambridge train station to check your bags and buy your London ticket, then drop off your empty car at the appropriate agency (see map). From there, take a taxi or one of many Market Square buses to the TI to get information and catch the city walk.

After dinner (or during dinner), the train will take you to London's Liverpool Street Station (at least hourly, about £7, 70 minutes). Hop onto London's handy Central subway line, and return to the hotel you reserved and paid for three weeks earlier.

There are very good direct bus connections from Cambridge to Heathrow and Gatwick airports (£7).

Cambridge

Sixty miles north of London, this historic town of 100,000 people is world famous for its prestigious university. Wordsworth, Isaac Newton, Tennyson, Darwin, and Prince Charles are a few products of this busy brain-works. Much more pleasant than its rival, Oxford, Cambridge is the epitome of a university town, with busy bikers, stately halls of residence, plenty of bookshops, and a fun youthfulness permeating its old walls.

Cambridge is small but very congested. There are two main streets separated from the river by the most interesting colleges. The town center has a handy TI, a colorful marketplace, and several parking lots. Everything is a pleasant walk away. Use the TI (Wheeler St., tel. 0223/322640, open Monday through Friday 9:00 a.m. to 6:00 p.m. or later; Saturday 9:00 a.m. to 5:00 p.m.; Sundays in summer 10:30 a.m. to 3:30 p.m.; good room-finding service). Remember, the university dominates—and owns—most of Cambridge. Approximate term schedule is January 15 through March 15, April 15 through June 8, and October 8 through December 8. The colleges are closed to visitors from May until late June. But the town is never sleepy.

Sightseeing Highlights

▲▲**Walking Tour of the Colleges**—The best way to understand Cambridge's town-gown rivalry and be sure to get a good rundown on the historic and scenic highlights of the university—as well as some fun local gossip—is to take the walking tour. It leaves from the TI at 11:00 a.m., 12:00 noon, 1:00 p.m., 2:00 p.m., and 3:00 p.m. in the summer (only at 2:00 p.m. in winter). Buy £2.50 tickets or call in reservations as early that day as you can (tickets must be picked up at least 30 minutes before your tour). If you miss a tour or want your own, private guides are usually on call, charging £25 for the two-hour walk. These tours do their best to include King's College Chapel and Trinity's Wren Library.

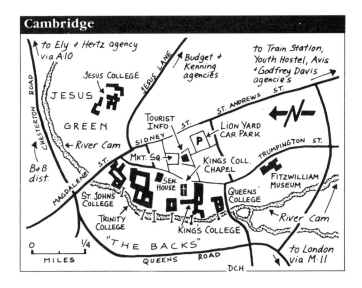

Cambridge

to Ely & Hertz agency via A-10
JESUS COLLEGE
JESUS LANE
CHESTERTON ROAD
JESUS
GREEN
← River Cam
B&B dist.
MAGDALENE ST.
Budget & Kenning agencies
TOURIST INFO
SIDNEY ST.
MKT. SQ.
ST. JOHNS COLLEGE
TRINITY COLLEGE
SEN. HOUSE
"THE BACKS"
KING'S COLLEGE
QUEENS ROAD
to Train Station, Youth Hostel, Avis & Godfrey Davis agencies
ST. ANDREWS ST.
LION YARD CAR PARK
KINGS COLL. CHAPEL
QUEENS COLLEGE
TRUMPINGTON ST.
FITZWILLIAM MUSEUM
River Cam
to London via M-11
0   ¼
MILES
DCH

▲▲**King's College Chapel**—View the most impressive single building in town, high Gothic at its best, with incredible fan vaulting and Rubens's great *Adoration of the Magi*. Open 9:30 a.m. to 5:45 p.m. daily except during school terms, when it's closed at 3:45 p.m. During term you're welcome to enjoy the 5:30 p.m. evensong service (Monday through Friday) at King's College Chapel.

▲▲**Trinity College**—The richest and biggest college here; don't miss its great courtyard or the Wren library with its wonderful carving and fascinating manuscripts. It's open Monday through Friday only, 12:00 noon to 2:00 p.m.

▲▲**Fitzwilliam Museum**—The best museum of antiquities and art outside of London, the Fitzwilliam has fine impressionist paintings, old manuscripts, and Greek, Egyptian, and Mesopotamian collections (antiquities open Tuesday through Saturday 10:00 a.m. to 2:00 p.m.; paintings, 2:00 p.m. to 5:00 p.m.; everything on Sunday 2:15 p.m. to 5:00 p.m.; closed Monday). Free and actually fun.

▲**Punting on the Cam**—For a little levity and probably

more exercise than you really want, try hiring one of the
traditional flat-bottom punts from stalls near either
bridge and pole yourself up and down (around and
around, more likely) the lazy Cam. Once you get the hang
of it, it's a fine way to enjoy the scenic side of Cambridge.
After 5:00 p.m. it's less crowded.

Accommodations

In case you decide to spend the night in Cambridge,
you'll be arriving early enough to find a room through
the TI.

Youth Hostel—The Cambridge hostel is modern,
easygoing, friendly, noisy, clean, and located near the
train station, a 20-minute walk from the center (cheap, 97
Tenison Rd., tel. 354601).

For nothing-special rooms in the nothing-special area
near the train station and the youth hostel, a 20-minute
walk from the center with plenty of bus connections
(down Hills Rd.), consider the **Westcote Guest House**
(inexpensive, especially in triples and quads, 33 Tenison
Rd., tel. 0223/62138, no lounge) and the **A & B Guest
House** (inexpensive, 124 Tenison Rd., tel. 0223/315702).

Good, very central B&Bs just north of Trinity College
are **Mrs. Patching** (mid-June through September, 10 Portugal St., tel. 355163), and **Mrs. Connally's B&B** (all
year, 67 Jesus Lane, tel. 61753).

Another good bet is **Netley Lodge B&B** (112 Chesterton Rd., Cambridge CB4 1B2, tel. 63845).

Itinerary Options

Cambridge is an easy day trip from London, about an
hour each way; round-trip rates are only a little more
than the one-way fare of about £7. The peaceful town of
Ely, with its knockout cathedral, is 20 minutes north of
busy Cambridge (TI tel. 0353/662062). If you opt for a
rest here before the bustle of London, stay at Mr. Green's
Black Hostelry, a medieval apartment right in the Cathedral Close courtyard and very quiet (moderate, tel.

0353/662612). The Ely youth hostel is in a downtown school building (tel. 667423).

Posttour London

Remember to call your airline to reconfirm your return flight three days in advance, leaving your London hotel's phone number for any messages.

Hopefully, you will have thought ahead, taking advantage of the opportunity to reserve hard-to-get tickets at the start of the trip to enjoy a special show or event before returning home.

Ask at your hotel for the easiest way to the airport. To Gatwick, take the shuttle train from Victoria Station. To Heathrow, take the subway or the Airbus. The Airbus is easier, dropping you right at the appropriate terminal (£5). Taxis are a rip-off from airports, but two or three people in a hurry can ride for a reasonable fare from the West End out. I flagged down a cab while waiting for the Airbus and negotiated a £15 ride from Holland Park to Heathrow.

Call before going out to the airport to check for delays. Call home (50p or £1 is enough) to say all's well and what time you're due in. You'll arrive home at almost the same time you left London, considering the hours you gain in westward flight.

The obvious gap in this 22-day plan is Ireland. I agonized over what to do with the friendly Emerald Isle. I love Ireland. Most who visit do. But it doesn't make Britain's top 22 days. Still, Ireland is easy to work in as a side trip or finale to this 22-day plan. Here are a few points to consider.

Itinerary Strategy—Getting There

Ireland can be inserted into the 22-day plan from North Wales. Boats sail from Holyhead to Dun Laoghaire (pronounced "dunleary") three or four times a day (4½-hour trip, $30, get ticket ASAP in London). Ask about cheap round-trip tickets. The train/boat London-Dublin ride costs about $50, overnight or all day. The London-Dublin bus fare is much cheaper. Buses go daily between Glasgow and Belfast (10 to 12 hours, $25). Flights from London to Dublin and Belfast are fairly cheap (around $100) and easy to arrange at any travel agency. Consider an "open-jaws" flight plan, flying into London and home from Shannon Airport in western Ireland. Your 22-day itinerary would then be: London, Wales, England, Scotland, Belfast, Dublin, West Ireland, home.

If you'll be touring the Continent with a Eurail pass, start it in Ireland (it's good on Irish trains and many buses) and ride free on the otherwise-expensive 24-hour boat ride to France. (Note: This ride can be rough. Upon boarding, those concerned about seasickness should go straight to the ship's cafeteria and eat a small plastic tub full of strawberry jelly. Although the jelly won't stop the nausea, it helps the aftertaste.)

Transportation in Ireland

For a quick visit to Dublin and a day tour into the countryside, you'll just ride the boat and catch a bus tour in Dublin. For a more extensive visit, here are your options. Irish trains are expensive and not extensive, with meager schedules and coverage. Britrail passes don't work here. The bus is cheaper and has a more extensive route system. Study special passes: students get a 50 percent discount with ISIC cards. Taking a car from England is complicated and expensive. Most people make arrangements from the U.S.A. to rent a car (by the week). Hitchhikers find Ireland easy to get around in, safe, and very friendly.

Suggested Itinerary

Day 1   Leave rental car at Holyhead, take boat to Dun Laoghaire, set up in Dublin.
Day 2   Sightsee Dublin.
Day 3   Side trip south to Glendalough and Wicklow Mountains.
Day 4   Early boat back to Holyhead, pick up car or train, and go to Blackpool.

Longer Ireland:

Revise your 22-day plan as if returning to London on the overnight train from Scotland (London-Bath-North Wales-York-Edinburgh). Turn in car in Edinburgh if driving.

Day 21 Edinburgh-Glasgow-Bus/Boat-Belfast.
Day 22 Sightsee in Belfast, afternoon at Cultra Folk Museum.
Day 23 Early train to Dublin, sightsee all day there.
Day 24 Dublin.
Day 25 Dublin-Cashel-Tralee-Dingle.
Day 26 Dingle, bike the peninsula.
Day 27 Dingle-Tralee-Shannon Airport to fly home; or, Dingle-Dublin, and night train/boat back to London.

Sightseeing Highlights

Dublin—Sooty Dublin, not a favorite city of mine, is nevertheless worth a day or two. The city center is compacted around O'Connell Street Bridge and the River Liffey. Boats land at nearby Dun Laoghaire with good bus connections into Dublin. (TI at 14 Upper O'Connell Street, tel. 747733, open Monday through Saturday 8:30 a.m. to 6:00 p.m., has good room-finding services. Orient yourself by taking a city walking tour.)

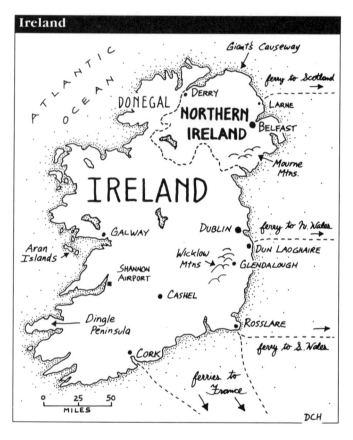

Ireland

ATLANTIC OCEAN

Giant's Causeway

ferry to Scotland →

DONEGAL

• DERRY

• LARNE

NORTHERN IRELAND

• BELFAST

Mourne Mtns.

IRELAND

ferry to N. Wales →

• GALWAY

DUBLIN •

• DUN LAOGHAIRE

Aran Islands

Wicklow Mtns →

• GLENDALOUGH

SHANNON AIRPORT

• CASHEL

Dingle Peninsula

• ROSSLARE →

ferry to S. Wales →

• CORK

ferries to France

0   25   50
MILES

DCH

Visit Trinity College (stately grounds, historic buildings,
illuminated Book of Kells manuscript); the National
Museum (moving Nathan Hale-type patriotism of the
martyrs of the 1916 Rebellion, impressive medieval and
earlier Irish artifacts, open Tuesday through Saturday
10:00 a.m. to 5:00 p.m., Sunday 2:00 p.m. to 5:00 p.m);
General Post Office (unimpressive building but the site of
the 1916 proclamation of the Independent Irish Republic); Kilmainham Jail (symbol of the Irish struggle against
Britain, martyr memorabilia, open Wednesday 10:00 a.m.
to 12:00 noon, 2:30 p.m. to 4:00 p.m., and Sunday 3:00
p.m. to 5:00 p.m. only); and the Guinness Brewery (video

show, free beer, Monday through Friday 10:00 a.m. to 5:00 p.m.).

For entertainment, sample the great Irish theater (Abbey Theater and many others, shows Monday through Saturday at 8:00 p.m.), seek out some Irish folk music in a local pub, or check out some Irish sports—hurling (the rugged national sport that's like airborne hockey with no injury time-outs) or Gaelic football (a violent form of rugby). Games are held nearly every Sunday at Dublin's Croke Park. Use the periodical entertainment guide called "In Dublin" for music, theater, sports, and tour listings.

Glendalough—The best short day trip from Dublin for a sample of rural Ireland is into the Wicklow mountains to Glendalough. Fifteen hundred years ago, the hermit St. Kevin established a thriving monastic school here. Today its ruins, surrounded by scenic forests and lakes, are understandably popular with tourists. Look into a one-day tour from Dublin.

Belfast—Just a direct three-hour train ride north, this embattled capital of the North offers a safe, fascinating look at "The Troubles." You'll be frisked at the checkpoint and then step into the traffic-free "safe zone." Browse through a bomb damage clearance sale. Take a side trip south to the wonderful Cultra Open-Air Folk Museum; talk to the people. With common sense (don't sing Catholic songs in Protestant pubs), Belfast is as safe as London. (See the chapter on Belfast in my book, *Europe Through the Back Door.*) Consider a Belfast-Glasgow bus connection.

Wexford-Rosslare Harbor—Visit this area only to catch the boat to South Wales or France.

Cork—Ireland's rough, but pleasant, second city. You can catch the boat to France (free on Eurail pass) here. The famous Blarney Castle with its too-famous Blarney Stone is nearby. Hordes of Americans smother it with kisses to get the "gift of gab"; local guys pee on it to get the gift of hilarity.

Cashel—This stirring religious and political center dates back to the mysterious days of St. Patrick. Fine Celtic cross graveyard, good tours. Open daily 9:00 a.m. to 7:30 p.m., 10:30 a.m. to 4:30 p.m. in winter. There are two buses daily to and from Dublin and Cork.

Dingle Peninsula—My favorite scenery in the British Isles is Ireland's West Coast, and the best in the west is the rugged beauty of hearty Dingle Peninsula, just north of the very touristy Ring of Kerry. Dingle is a Gaeltacht—a region where the locals still speak the old Irish or Gaelic language. This is a cultural preserve with traditional dress, music, and life-styles complementing the natural beauty. (See *Europe Through the Back Door* chapter on Dingle.) Train to the pleasant town of Tralee, then bus or thumb to Dingle town. Set up at Mrs. Farrell's Corner House (tel. 066/51516). Rent a bike for the circular trip out to Slea Head (closest point to the U.S., incredible scenery, villages; explore the medieval monks' stone beehive huts, or *clochans*, along the way), but be home in time to catch the nightly folk music at O'Flaherty's Pub.

For a more peaceful home base, the **Skellig View B&B** (1 mile east of Ventry, outside of Dingle town, run by Eileen and Paddy Cleary) is great.

Galway—The largest city in western Ireland, coastal Galway is cozy, historic, and 3½ hours by train to and from Dublin and Cork (direct bus service to Rosslare, a ferry port). Daily boats and cheap flights to the Aran Islands (try for any kind of discount you can dream up).

Aran Islands—Off the coast of Galway, this tiny group of wave-whipped islands is a stark, stubborn outpost of old Irish culture and not terribly touristy. Spend two days on the main island, rent bikes, and explore. Boats connect islands with the mainland. One goes to Doolin, home of Ireland's best folk music but not much else.

Donegal—Ireland in the extreme, Donegal is the cultural Yukon of this lush island, where everyone seems to be typecast for an Irish movie. Enter Donegal with caution, for while it has no real "sights," it is seductive, and many unwary visitors end up skipping the rest of their itinerary. One Arizona accountant "called in well" and was never seen again.

Helpful Hints

Understand Ireland's "Troubles"—the North-South, Catholic-Protestant problem. A fine background and wonderful reading is *Trinity* by Leon Uris.

Ireland is very small (about 150 miles by 200 miles), but it has no English-style motorways. Transportation is slow. Approach every trip as a joyride. Traveling in Ireland is generally cheaper than in England. The Irish pound is worth a little less than the British pound.

Ireland's B&Bs are even cozier and less expensive than England's, and traveling without reservations is not difficult. Use the *Let's Go: Britain and Ireland* guidebook. Ireland's weather ranges from damp to drizzly to downpour, and her people are her main attraction. You can't enjoy Ireland without enjoying her people.

APPENDIX

22 DAYS IN GREAT BRITAIN BY TRAIN AND BUS

Britain has a great train and bus system, and travelers who don't want to (or can't afford to) drive a rental car can enjoy 22 exciting days using public transportation. But you'll lose a lot of control, and Britain, more than any other European country, lends itself to car travel.

A train/bus trip requires some tailoring to avoid areas that are difficult to get to without your own wheels and to take advantage of certain bonuses train travel offers. Consider a plan such as this one:

Britain by Train in 22 Days

Day 1	Arrive in London.
Day 2	London.
Day 3	London.
Day 4	Bath.
Day 5	Side trip to Wells and Glastonbury.
Day 6	Cardiff, St. Fagans, to Cheltenham.
Day 7	Explore Cotswolds with Cheltenham as a base.
Day 8	Stratford, Warwick.
Day 9	Coventry to North Wales.
Day 10	North Wales.
Day 11	North Wales-Blackpool.
Day 12	Blackpool-York.
Day 13	York.
Day 14	York-Durham-Hadrian's Wall-Edinburgh.
Day 15	Edinburgh.
Day 16	Edinburgh.
Day 17	Edinburgh-Mallaig.
Day 18	Isle of Skye-Inverness, night train to London.
Day 19	London—side trip to Cambridge.
Day 20	Side trip from London to Salisbury, Stonehenge.
Day 21	Free day.
Day 22	Free day to insert where needed.

London is the hub, with speedy commuter trains going everywhere. Remember, London has many stations, each serving a general region. Round-trip "day return" tickets are just a bit more expensive than one-way fares, making day trips to places such as Cambridge, Salisbury, Stonehenge, Oxford, Stratford, and Bath reasonable: London to Salisbury (80 miles from Waterloo Station, 90 minutes, hourly); Salisbury to Stonehenge (9 miles, 30-minute bus ride changing at Amesbury, several a day from downtown or station); London to Bath (from Paddington Station, 70 minutes, hourly). For London train information to Scotland and the North, call 278-2477; to the Midlands and North Wales, call 387-7070; and to West England and South Wales, call 262-6767. Note: All times and schedules listed work the same in both directions.

Bath—Most larger journeys change at Bristol (15 minutes from Bath, four times an hour).

Bristol to Cardiff (60 minutes, hourly)—Bath train information, tel. 463075; coach information, tel. 464446.

Cardiff—The transportation hub of South Wales. Buses direct to St. Fagan's and Caerphilly. Train to Cheltenham (80 minutes, every two hours). Train information, tel. 228000; bus information, tel. 371331.

Cheltenham—The Cotswolds are hiking, biking, or driving country, but a few train lines and sporadic bus service will get you around if necessary. Cheltenham, from a public transportation point of view, is your best home base. Be sure to pick up the *Cotswold Bus and Rail Guide* there. Cheltenham-Birmingham (hourly, 45-minute rides). Train information, tel. 0452/29501; bus information, tel. 22021; Cheltenham TI, tel. 522878.

Stratford-Warwick-Coventry—This segment of the trip is easy by car but messy otherwise. Birmingham is the transportation hub of this region, and each place is well served from Birmingham: Stratford to Warwick (train and bus almost hourly, 20-minute ride), to Coventry (bus almost hourly, 75-minute ride), to London (eight trains a day, two hours). Train information, tel. 021/643 2711; bus information, tel. 021/622 4373. Tour companies make

BritRail Routes

KEY: * MAP NOT TO SCALE

LONDON AIRPORTS: A-HEATHROW B-GATWICK

LONDON STATIONS:

1 **VICTORIA** - S. & S.E. ENG., CONNECTIONS TO PARIS & BRUSSELS
2 **CHARING CROSS** - S.E. ENG.
3 **WATERLOO** - S. ENGLAND.
4 **LIVERPOOL ST.** - EAST ANGLIA, AMSTERDAM   CONNECTIONS TO
5 **KING'S CROSS** - MIDLANDS, N.E. ENG., E. SCOTLAND
6 **ST. PANCRAS** - E. MIDLANDS
7 **EUSTON** - MIDLANDS, N. WALES, N.W. ENG., W. SCOT
8 **PADDINGTON** - W. ENG, S. WALES

—— RAIL --- BUS
···· FERRY WITH
(6H) CROSSING TIME

NOTE: FASTER ENGLISH
CHANNEL CROSSINGS WITH
HOVERCRAFT & HYDROFOIL
ON SOME RUNS. CHECK!

DCH

day-tripping from Stratford to Blenheim, Oxford, the Cotswolds, Warwick, and Coventry possible—but not cheap.

Coventry—Bus #25 connects the bus and train stations going through the center of town past the cathedral and TI. National Express (tel. 021/622 4373) offers 12-hour day trips from London to Coventry and Warwick for £10.

Ironbridge Gorge—This birthplace of the Industrial Revolution is still in the Stone Age, transportation-wise. You can train to Wellington and catch a bus to Ironbridge Gorge from there, but I'd consider skipping the entire area. (Use Conwy or Bangor as your home base.)

North Wales—The plan in this book won't work without a car, but North Wales has good and scenic trains and buses. You can pick up plenty of information locally, and a special Day Rover ticket gives you a day of buses for only £3. Chester-Holyhead train (about seven times a day, two hours). Caenarfon-Blaenau Ffestiniog (bus every two hours). Look into the old miniature-gauge Ffestiniog railroad.

Chester-Crew-Preston-Blackpool—This is England's industrial heartland, and trains are very frequent. With the two changes, this journey should take three hours.

Blackpool-Manchester (two per hour, 90-minute ride).

Manchester-York (leaving at 28 minutes past each hour, 90-minute ride).

Lake District—Frustrating for those with limited time and no car. There are buses and trains serving the area, but, without a car, I'd skip it.

York and Edinburgh are very well connected by train (hourly trips, 2½ hours). That train stops in Durham and Newcastle. York-London (hourly, two hours long). York train information, tel. 0904/64 21 55; bus information, tel. 0532/460011. There is a special bus from Durham directly to the nearby Beamish folk museum.

Durham-Newcastle (four trains per hour, 15 minutes)—Tour Hadrian's Wall from Newcastle. The Newcastle-

Carlisle train is very scenic, stopping at Hexham and Halt-
whistle and going right along the wall (hourly, 90-minute
ride). In the summer there's a tourist-oriented bus service
four times a day from Newcastle.

Edinburgh—To get to the rugged west and islands
from Edinburgh, you go via Glasgow (trains from Edinburgh twice an hour, 50 minutes) or Inverness (four times
a day, 3 ½ hours). Edinburgh has plenty of reasonably
priced organized bus tours covering Loch Ness, Oban,
Isle of Mull, and Inverness. Glasgow-Oban train (three
hours, three a day), Glasgow-Mallaig (six hours with an
hour break in Fort William, three a day), Kyle of
Lochalsh-Inverness (2 ½ hours, three a day). Edinburgh
train information, tel. 556-2451; bus information, tel.
556-8464. In Scotland, reservations are advisable in the
summertime.

Overnight Train Back to London: Inverness-
London/Euston (7:35 p.m. to 6:36 a.m., 8:50 p.m. to 8:14
a.m. each night), a sleeping berth (£18) is a good invest-
ment. Inverness train information, tel. 0463/23 89 24;
bus information, tel. 233371.

A trip of this. . . ferocity. . . justifies a BritRail Pass.
These passes give you unlimited rail travel in England,
Scotland, and Wales. You must buy it outside of Great
Britain (ideally, from your travel agent). The promotional
information is a bit complicated but very thorough. Read
it carefully.

BritRail Pass Rates (1991)					Flexipass	
	8 days	15 days	22 days	1 month	4 in 8	8 in 15
Youth (under 26)	169	255	319	375	145	199
Economy	209	319	399	465	179	255
First Class	319	479	599	689	289	379
Senior Economy (over 60)	189	289	359	419	159	229

For more information, including a British Rail network map, write to your nearest BritRail Travel International Office:

■1500 Broadway, New York, NY 10036, (212) 575-2667 or 1-800-677-8585.

■94 Cumberland Street, Suite 601, Toronto M5R 1A3, ON, (416) 929-3334

■409 Granville Street, Vancouver V6C 1T2, BC, (604) 683-6896

British buses are cheaper but slower than trains. They will take you where the trains won't. Stations are often at or near train stations. The British distinguish between "buses" (for local runs with lots of stops) and "coaches" (long distance, express runs). If your budget is very tight, you can save money by skipping the BritRail Pass in favor of buses.

Of course, you could do this whole trip hitchhiking. It would take more time, but you'd make a lot more friends. If you plan to ride your thumb, get a hitching guidebook (try *Hitch Hikers Manual: Britain*, from Vacation Work, 9 Park End St., Oxford OX1 IHJ, or *A Hitch-hiker's Guide to Great Britain*, published by Penguin Books).

WHAT'S SO GREAT ABOUT BRITAIN?

Regardless of the revolution we had 200 years ago, Americans "go home" to Britain. This most popular tourist destination has a strange influence and power over us.

Britain is small—about the size of Uganda (or Idaho)—600 miles tall and 300 miles at its widest. Its highest mountain is 4,400 feet—a foothill by our standards. The population is a quarter of the U.S.A.'s, and, politically and economically, the Great Britain closing out the twentieth century is only a weak shadow of the days when it boasted, "The sun never sets on the British Empire."

At one time, Britain owned one-fifth of the world and accounted for more than half the planet's industrial output. Today, the Empire is down to tidbits such as the Falklands and Northern Ireland, and Great Britain's industrial production is about 5 percent of the world's total.

Still, Britain is a world leader. Her heritage, her culture, and her people cannot be measured in traditional units of power. The United Kingdom is a union of four countries—England, Wales, Scotland, and Northern Ireland. Cynics call it an English Empire ruled by London, and there is some tension between the dominant Anglo-Saxon English (46 million) and their Celtic brothers (10 million).

In the Dark Ages, the Angles moved into this region from Europe, pushing the Celtic inhabitants to the undesirable fringe of the islands. The Angles settled in Angle-land (England), while the Celts made do in Wales, Scotland, and Ireland.

Today, Wales, with 2 million people, struggles along with a terrible economy, dragged down by the depressed mining industry. A great deal of Welsh pride is apparent in the local music and the bilingual signs. Fifty thousand people speak Welsh.

Scotland is big, accounting for one-third of Great Britain's land area, but is sparsely inhabited, by only 5 million people. Only about 80,000 speak Gaelic, but the Scots enjoy a large measure of autonomy with their separate Church of Scotland, their own legal system, and Scottish currency.

Ireland, the island west of England, is divided. Most of it is the completely independent and Catholic Republic of Ireland. The top quarter is Northern Ireland—ruled from London. Long ago, the Protestant English and Scots moved into the north, the industrial heartland of Ireland, and told the Catholic Irish to "go to Hell or go to Connemara." They moved to the bleak and less productive parts of the island, like Connemara, and the seeds of today's "Troubles" were planted. There's no easy answer or easy blame, but that island has struggled—its population is only a third (3 million) of what it used to be—and the battle continues. As a visitor today, you'll see a politically polarized England. The Conservatives are taking a

Reaganesque approach to Britain's serious problems, returning to Victorian values—community, family, hard work, thrift, and trickle-down. The Labor and Liberal parties see an almost irreparable break-up of the social service programs so dear to them and so despised by those with much to conserve.

Basic British History for the Traveler
When Julius Caesar landed on the misty and mysterious isle of Britain in 55 B.C., England entered the history books. The primitive Celtic tribes he conquered were themselves invaders who had earlier conquered the even more mysterious people who built Stonehenge in pre-historic times.

The Romans built towns and roads (including Icknield Way and Foss Way, which remain today) and established their capital at "Londinium." The Celtic natives, consisting of Gaels, Picts, and Scots, were not subdued so easily in Scotland and Wales, so the Romans built Hadrian's Wall near the Scottish border to keep invading Scots out. Even today, the Celtic language and influence are strongest in the Gaelic and Scottish regions. As Rome fell, so fell Roman Britain—a victim of invaders and internal troubles. Barbarian tribes from Germany and Denmark called Angles and Saxons swept through the southern part of the island, establishing Angle-land. These were the days of the real King Arthur, probably a Christianized Roman general fighting valiantly but in vain against invading barbarians. The island was plunged into 500 years of Dark Ages—wars, plagues, and poverty—lit only by the dim candle of a few learned Christian monks and missionaries trying to convert the barbarians.

Modern England began with yet another invasion. William the Conquerer and his Norman troops crossed the channel from France in 1066. William crowned himself king in Westminster Abbey (where all subsequent coronations would take place) and began building the Tower of London. French-speaking Norman kings ruled the country for two centuries. Then the country suffered through two centuries of civil wars, with various noble families vying for the crown. In one of the most bitter feuds, the York and Lancaster families fought the War of the Roses, so-called because of the white and red flowers they chose as their symbols. Battles, intrigues, kings, nobles, and ladies imprisoned and executed in the Tower—it's a wonder the country survived its rulers.

England was finally united by the "third-party" Tudor family. Henry VIII, a Tudor, was England's Renaissance king. He was handsome, athletic, a poet, a scholar, and a musician. He was also arrogant, cruel, gluttonous, and paranoid. He went through six wives in 40 years, divorcing, imprisoning, or beheading them when they no longer suited his needs. Henry also "divorced" England from the Catholic church, establishing the Protestant Church of England (Anglican church) and setting in motion years of religious squabbles. Henry also "dissolved" the monasteries, leaving just the shells of many formerly glorious abbeys dotting the countryside.

Henry's daughter, Queen Elizabeth I, made England a great naval and trading power and presided over the Elizabethan era of great writers, including Shakespeare.

The long-standing quarrel between England's kings and nobles in Parliament finally erupted into a Civil War (1643). Parliament forces under the Puritan farmer Oliver Cromwell defeated—and beheaded—King Charles I. This Civil War left its mark on much of what you'll see in England. Eventually, Parliament invited Charles's son to retake the throne. This restoration of the monarchy was accompanied by a great rebuilding of London (including Christopher Wren's St. Paul's Cathedral), which had been devastated by the Great Fire of 1666.

Britain grew as a great naval power, colonizing and trading with all parts of the globe. Her naval superiority ("Britannia rules the waves") was secured by Admiral Nelson's victory over Napoleon's fleet at the Battle of Trafalgar, while Lord Wellington stomped Napoleon on land at Waterloo. Nelson and Wellington are memorialized by many arches, columns, squares, and so on, throughout England.

Economically, Britain led the world into the Industrial Age with her mills, factories, coal mines, and trains. By the time of Queen Victoria's reign (1837-1901), Britain was at the zenith of power with a colonial empire that covered one-fifth of the world. The twentieth century has not been kind to Britain, however. Two World Wars devastated the population. The Nazi Blitz reduced much of London to rubble. Her colonial empire has dwindled to almost nothing, and she is no longer an economic superpower. The "Irish Troubles" are a constant thorn as the Catholic inhabitants of British-ruled Northern Ireland fight for the same independence their southern neighbors won decades ago. The recent war over the Falkland Islands showed how little of the British Empire is left but also how determined the British are to hang onto what remains.

The tradition of greatness continues unbowed, however, presided over by Queen Elizabeth II, her husband Prince Phillip, the heir-apparent Prince Charles and his wife, Lady Di. The pomp and circumstance surrounding the wedding of Prince Andrew and Sarah Ferguson shows how much the trappings of the monarchy mean to the British people.

Architecture in Britain
From Stonehenge to Big Ben, travelers are going to be storming castle walls, climbing spiral staircases, and snapping the pictures of 5,000 years of architecture. Let's sort it out.

The oldest stuff—mysterious and prehistoric—goes from before Roman times back to 3000 B.C. The earliest—such as Stonehenge and Avebury—is from the Stone and Bronze ages. The remains from this period are made of huge stones or mounds of earth, even man-made hills, and were built for worship or burial. Iron Age people (600 B.C. to A.D. 43) left us desolate stone forts. The Romans thrived in Britain from A.D. 50 to 400, building cities, walls, and roads. Evidence of Roman greatness can be seen in lavish villas with ornate mosaic floors, temples uncovered beneath great English churches, and Roman stones in medieval city walls. Roman roads sliced across the island in straight lines. Today, any unusually straight small rural road is very likely laid directly on an ancient Roman road.

Roman Britain crumbled in the fifth century, and there was little building in Dark Age England. Architecturally, the light was switched on with the Norman Conquest in 1066. As William earned his title "the Conquerer," he built churches and castles in the European Romanesque style.

English Romanesque is called "Norman." The round arches and strong, simple, and stocky Norman style (1050-1200) made for churches that were fortresslike, with thick walls, small windows, and crenellations. Durham Cathedral and the Chapel of St. John in the Tower of London are typical Norman churches. The Tower of London, with its square keep, small windows, and spiral stone stairways, is a typical Norman castle. You'll see plenty of Norman castles—all built to secure the conquest of these invaders from Normandy.

Gothic architecture (1200-1600) replaced the heavy Norman style with light, vertical buildings, pointed arches, tall soaring spires, and bigger windows. English Gothic is divided into three stages. Early English (1200-1300) features tall, simple spires, beautifully carved capitals, and elaborate chapter houses (such as Salisbury and Wells cathedrals). Decorated Gothic (1300-1370) gets fancier with more elaborate tracery, bigger windows, and ornately carved pinnacles, as you'll see at Westminster Abbey. Finally, the perpendicular style (1370-1600) goes back to square towers and emphasizes straight, uninter-rupted, vertical lines from ceiling to floor with vast win-dows and exuberant decoration including fan-vaulted ceilings (King's College Chapel at Cambridge).

As you tour the great medieval churches of England, remember, nearly everything is symbolic. Local guides give regular tours, and books also help us modern pil-grims understand at least a little of what we see. For instance, on the tombs, if the figure has crossed legs, he was a crusader. If his feet rest on a dog, he died at home, but if the legs rest on a lion, he died in battle.

Wales is particularly rich in castles. The rulers seem to have needed castles to subdue the stubborn Welsh. Edward I built a ring of powerful castles in Wales (such as Caernarfon and Conway) to deal with the Welsh.

Gothic houses were a simple mix of woven strips of thin wood, rubble, and plaster called wattle and daub. The famous black-and-white Tudor, or half-timbered, look was simply heavy oak frames filled in with the wattle and daub.

The Tudor period (1485-1560) was a time of relative peace (the War of the Roses was finally over), prosperity, and renaissance. Henry VIII broke with the Catholic church and "dissolved" (destroyed) the monasteries, leaving scores of England's greatest churches gutted shells. These hauntingly beautiful abbey ruins surrounded by lush lawns (Glastonbury, Tintern, Whitby) are now pleasant city parks. York's magnificent Minster survived only because Henry needed an administrative headquarters in the North for his Anglican church.

Although few churches were built, this was a time of house and mansion construction. Warmth was becoming popular and affordable, and Tudor buildings featured small square windows and often many chimneys. In towns where land was scarce, many Tudor houses grew up and out, getting wider with each overhanging floor.

The Elizabethan and Jacobean periods (1560-1620) were followed by the English Renaissance style (1620-1720). English architects mixed Gothic and classical styles, then baroque and classical styles. Although the ornate baroque never really grabbed England, the classical style of the Italian architect, Palladio, did. Inigo Jones (1573-1652), Christopher Wren (1632-1723), and those they inspired plastered England with enough columns, domes, and symmetry to please a Caesar. The Great Fire of London (1666) paved the way for an ambitious young Wren to put his mark on London forever with a grand rebuilding scheme including the great St. Paul's and more than 50 other churches.

The Georgian period (1720-1840), featuring the lousy German kings of England whom the celebrants of the Boston tea party couldn't stand, was rich and showed its richness by being very classical. Grand pedimental doorways, fine cast iron work on balconies and railings, Chippendale furniture, and white-on-blue Wedgewood ceramics graced rich homes everywhere. John Wood, Jr. and Sr., led the way, giving the trend-setting city of Bath its crescents and circles of royal Georgian rowhouses.

The Industrial Revolution shaped the Victorian period (1840-1890) with glass, steel, and iron. England had a huge new erector set (so did France's Mr. Eiffel). This was also a romantic period, reviving the "more Christian" Gothic style. London's Houses of Parliament are neo-Gothic—just 100 years old but looking 700 except for the telltale modern precision and craftsmanship. Whereas Gothic was stone or concrete, neo-Gothic was often red brick. These were England's glory days, and there was more building in this period than in all previous ages combined.

The architecture of our century obeys the formula "form follows function"—it works well but isn't particularly interesting. England treasures its heritage and takes great pains to build tastefully in historic districts and to preserve its many "listed" buildings. With a booming tourist trade, these quaint reminders of its—and our—past are becoming a valuable part of the British economy.

British TV
British television is so good—and so British—that it deserves a mention as a sightseeing treat (especially after a hard day of castle climbing) over a pot of tea in the comfortable living room of your village bed and breakfast.

England has four channels. BBC 1 and BBC 2 are government run, commercial-free, and rather highbrow. ITV and Channel 4 are private, a little more Yankee, and have commercials—but those commercials are clever, sophisticated, and a fun look at England. The public channels are funded by a $175-per-year-per-TV tax. Hmmm, 50 cents per day to escape commercials. Whereas California "accents" fill our airwaves 24 hours a day, homogenizing the way our country speaks, England protects and promotes its regional accents by its choice of announcers. Commercial-free British TV is looser than it used to be but is still careful about what it airs when.

American shows are very popular—especially *Hill Street Blues, Cheers, Cagney and Lacey, Dallas,* and *Dynasty.* Oldies such as *Bewitched* and *I Dream of Jeannie* are also broadcasted. The visiting viewer should be sure to tune in a few typical English shows. I'd recommend a dose of English situation and political comedy fun (*Yes, Minister, Spitting Image*) and the topnotch BBC evening news. For a tear-filled taste of British soap, see the popular *Coronation Street* or *Eastenders*, and, for an English Johnny Carson, see Terry Wogan's comedy show.

And, of course, if you like the crazy, offbeat Benny Hill and Monty Python-type comedy, you've come to the right place.

TELEPHONE DIRECTORY

City	Area Code/ Tourist Info	Train Info
London	071/730-3488	
Salisbury	0722/334956	27591
Bath	0225/462831	463075
Cardiff	0222/227281	228000
Stow-on-the-Wold	0451/31082	
Wells	0749/72552	
Stratford	0789/293127	091/22302
Coventry	0203/832312	6432711
Iron Bridge Gorge	095245/2753	
Ruthin, N. Wales	08242/3992	
Blackpool	0772/21623	59439
Windermere	09662/6499	
Keswick	07687/72645	0539/33231
Oban	0631/63122	63083

Inverness	0463/234353	238924
Edinburgh	031/557-1700	556-2451
Durham	091/3843720	2326262
York	0904/621756	642155
Cambridge	0223/322640	311999
Dublin	01/747733	366222

To dial the U.S.A.: 010—1 (country code)—area code—seven-digit number. Costs about £1/minute, cheaper after 6:00 p.m. and on weekends. In the U.S.A. it is five hours (East Coast) to eight hours (West Coast) earlier than in England. A five-second phone call costs only about 20p.

| Operator | 100 | London Dir. Assist. | 142 |
| Emergency | 999 | Dir. Ass. Outside London | 192 |

International code 010

U.S.A.	1	Germany	49
Canada	1	Italy	39
Belgium	32	Netherlands	31
France	33	Switzerland	41

Weather report, Lake District—09662/5151
Airport information: Heathrow 071/759-4321 or 745-7067, Gatwick 0293/28822
U.S.Embassy: 071/499/9000
AT&T "U.S.A. direct": 0800-8900-11
MCI "U.S.A. direct": 0800-89-02-22

WEIGHTS AND MEASURES

1 imperial gallon = 1.2 U.S. gallons or about 5 liters
1 stone = 14 lbs. (a 175 lb. person weighs 12 stone)
1 mile = 1.6 kilometers. 1 kilometer = 6/10 mile
Shoe sizes—about ½ to 1½ sizes smaller than in U.S. Ask!

BRITISH-YANKEE VOCABULARY

British/American
banger   sausage
biscuit   cookie
bloke   man, guy
bonnet   car hood
boot   car trunk
brilliant   nfty
candy floss   cotton candy
cheers   good-bye or thanks
chemist   pharmacy
chips   French fries
crisps   potato chips
dicey   iffy, questionable
dinner   lunch
dual carriageway   four-lane highway
fag   cigarette
faggot   meatball
first floor   second floor
fortnight   two weeks
give way   yield
half eight   8:30 (not 7:30)
hoover   vacuum cleaner
iron monger   hardware store
jumble   sale rummage sale
jumper   sweater
knickers   underpants
knock up   wake up or visit
loo   bathroom
lorry   truck
motorway   highway
nackered   dead tired
nosh   food
off license   can sell take-away liquor
take away   to go
petrol   gas
pillar box   postbox
queue up   line up

randy   horny
ring up   call (telephone)
rubber   eraser
single ticket   one-way ticket
stone   14 lbs. weight
sweets   candy
serviette   napkin
solicitor   lawyer
subway   underground pedestrian passageway
sweets   candy
telly   TV
to let   for rent
torch   flashlight
underground   subway
verge   edge of road
wellingtons, wellies   rubber boots
zebra crossing   crosswalk
zed   the letter "z"

INDEX

Accommodations 3, 13-16
  see also Food and Lodging
Activities (in 22 Days itinerary
  order)
  London Walk 41, 44
  Auction at Christie's 51
  Ultimate Pub Crawl 53
  Ceremony of Keys, Tower of
    London 55
  Bath Walks 61
  Bike the Cotswolds 78
  Medieval Banquet,
    Ruthin 87
  Tour Slate Mine 93
  Hiking in Lakes District
    102-103, 107-108
  Great Pool, Edinburgh 127
  Greyhound Races,
    Edinburgh 127
  York Walks 141
Bath, accommodations 63-65
Beatles 99
Bed and breakfasts 13-15
Beer, British 18
Bomb damage clearance
  sale 153
Bonnie Prince Charlie 115
Britain, background 161-169
  architecture 165-168
  history 163-165
  "Irish Troubles" 165
  TV 168-169
Buses, British 161
Captain Cook 134-135
Car, drop in Cambridge 145
  insurance 12
  or train 11
  rental 11-12
Churchill 77

Climate 7
Cost, trip 2-3
Driving British 12-13
Durham, accommo-
  dations 134
Eating in Britain 16-18
Edinburgh 117-129
  accommodations 119-122
  Edinburgh Castle 124
  Edinburgh Festival 128
  folk music 129
  Royal Mile 124
  sightseeing highlights
    124-129
England
  Avebury stone circle 58
  Bamburgh 133
  Bath 61-69
  Beamish Open-Air
    Museum 132-133
  Beatrix Potter's farm 102
  Bibury 77
  Blackpool 95-98
  Blenheim Palace 77
  Bourton-on-the-Water 76
  Broadway 76
  Cambridge 146-148
  Castle Howard 137
  Castlerigg Stone Circle 108
  Chester 98
  Chipping Campden 76
  Cotswolds 71-78
  Coventry's Cathedral 82
  Cumbrian Lake
    District 100-108
  Derwent Water 107
  Dove Cottage, Wordsworth's
    106-107
  Durham, Cathedral 133

Ely   148
Glastonbury   68
Hadrian's Wall   130-132
Hidcote Manor   77
Holy Island   133
Keswick   106
Liverpool   98-99
London   27-55
North York Moors   136-137
Nuclear Power Plant, Sella-
    field   108
Salisbury   58
Severn River Valley   84
Sherwood Forest   144-145
Staithes   134-135
Stonehenge   58
Stow-on-the-Wold   71-78
Stratford-upon-Avon   79-81
Ullswater   102
Warwick Castle   81-82
Wells   67-68
Winchester   58-59
Windermere Lake District
    100-108
Woodstock   77
Wookey Hole   66-67
York   137-143
Flying to London   11
Food and Lodging (in 22 Days
    itinerary order)
    London   34-41
    Bath   63-65
    Stow-on-the-Wold   71-73
    Ironbridge Gorge   82-83
    Ruthin   88-90
    Blackpool   98
    Lakes District   103-104
    Oban, Scotland   111-112
    Edinburgh   119-123
    Durham   134-135
    York   138-140
Guidebooks, recommended
    8-10

Heart attack, on a plate   16
Herriot, James   137
Highlands, Scottish   113-115
Hike, Lakes District   107-108
Holy Island   133
Hood, Robin, and his Merry
    Men   144
Hotels   13
    see also Food and Lodging
Industrial Revolution   84-86
Ireland   150-155
    Aran Islands   154
    Belfast   153
    Cashel   153-154
    Cork   153
    Dingle Peninsula   154
    Donegal   154-155
    Dublin   151-153
    Galway   154
    "Irish Troubles"   155
    suggested itinerary   151
Ironbridge Gorge   82-87
    accommodations   82-83
Itinerary, overview   22-26
Jet lag, minimize   27-28
London   27-55
    accommodations   34-38
    arrival in   28-29
    day trips from   54
    entertainment and
        theater   52-53
    food   38-41
    information   32-33
    posttour   149
    sightseeing highlights
        43-52
    transportation in   30-32
Maps (in 22 Days itinerary
    order)
    22 Days in Great Britain   iv
    Tour Route: 22 Days in
        Britain   23
    Landing at Heathrow
        3, 28

Leaving Heathrow   29
London, Our Neighbor-
    hood   35
London, The Underground
    46
Central London   47
Bath   62
London to Bath and South
    Wales   67
Cotswold Villages   76
Cotswold to Ironbridge   81
Ironbridge Gorge   85
Ruthin   86
North Wales   92
Blackpool   96
Cumbrian Lake District,
    Windermere   101
Scotland   110
Oban   111
Edinburgh Center   118
Edinburgh, Our Neighbor-
    hood   121
Edinburgh-Hadrian's Wall-
    Durham   131
York: Our Neighborhood
    139
York   142
Cambridge   147
Ireland   152
Britrail Routes   158
Meals   3, 16-18
    see also Food and Lodging
Money, British   4-5
Philosophy, Back Door   21
Pubs   17-18
Pub grub   17-18
Roman Britain
    Cirencester   75
    Hadrian's Wall   132
Royal Shakespeare
    Company   80-81
Ruthin   87-94
    accommodations   88-89

medieval banquet   87-88
Scotland
    Ben Nevis   114
    Caledonian Canal   114
    Culloden Battlefield   115
    Edinburgh   117-129
    Findhorn Foundation   115
    Glencoe   114
    Highlands, Scottish   113-115
    Iona, island   110
    Isle of Mull   110
    Loch Ness   113, 114-115
    Oban   110-112
    Pitlochry   115
Scottish words   116
Shakespeare's birthplace   79
Slate mining   93-94
Stow, eating in   72-73
Tax, value added, refunds   4
Telephoning   7-8
    directory   169-170
Three-star attractions (in 22
    Days itinerary order)
    Tower of London   44-45
    Westminster   45, 48
    British Museum   50
    The Baths of Bath   61
    Walking Tours of Bath   61
    Costume Museum   61
    Welsh Folk Museum at
        St. Fagan's   70
    Blenheim Palace   77
    Ironbridge Gorge Industrial
        Revolution Museums
        84-86
    Ullswater Hike and Boat
        Ride   102
    Royal Mile, Edinburgh   124
    The Edinburgh Festival
        128-129
    Hadrian's Wall   132
    The York Minster
        (cathedral)   142

York Castle Museum   143
Tourist Information
  Centres   10
  telephone numbers   169-170
Train, 22 Day Plan   156-161
  information, telephone
     numbers   169-170
  travel in Britain   156-161
Traveler's checks   5
Ugly Americanism   18-19
Vocabulary, British-Yankee
  171-172
Wales
  North Wales   87-94
     Betws-y-Coed   92-93
     Caernarfon Castle   93
     Llangollen   87
     Llechweld Slate Mine
        Tour   93
     Ruthin   87-94
     Snowdonia National Park
        92-93
     Woolen Mills, Trefriw   93

South Wales, Wye River
  Valley   69-71
  Caerphilly Castle   71
  Cardiff   69-70
  Forest of Dean   69, 70
  Gower Peninsula   73
  St. Briavals Castle   73
  St. Fagan's Welsh Folk
     Museum   69-70
  Tintern Abbey ruins
     69, 71
Weather   6-7
Weetabix   16
Weights and measures,
  Britain   170
Welsh language   94
Wordsworth Country
  100-108
York   137-143
  accommodations   138-140
  Railroad Museum   141-142
Youth Hostels   15-16
  see also Food and Lodging

Rick Steves'   BACK DOOR CATALOG

*All items field tested, highly recommended, completely guaran-
teed, discounted below retail and ideal for independent, mobile
travelers. Prices include tax (if applicable), handling, and postage.*

The Back Door Suitcase / Rucksack $65.00

At 9"x22"x14" this specially designed, sturdy functional
bag is maximum carry-on-the-plane size (fits under the
seat) and your key to foot-loose and fancy-free travel.
Made of rugged water resistant Cordura nylon, it converts
easily from a smart-looking suitcase to a handy rucksack.
It has hide-away padded shoulder straps, top and side
handles and a detachable shoulder strap (for toting as a
suitcase). Lockable perimeter zippers allow easy access to
the roomy (2,700 cubic inches) central compartment. Two large outside
pockets are perfect for frequently used items. Also included are three net
nylon stuff bags. Over 25,000 Back Door travelers have used these bags
around the world. Rick Steves helped design and lives out of this bag for 3
months at a time. Comparable bags cost much more. Available in navy blue,
black, grey, or burgundy.

Moneybelt $8.00

This required, ultra-light, sturdy, under-the-pants, nylon
pouch just big enough to carry the essentials (passport, airline ticket, travelers checks, and so on) comfortably. I'll
never travel without one and I hope you won't either. Beige,
nylon zipper, one size fits nearly all, with "manual."

Catalog   FREE

For a complete listing of all the books, travel class videos,
products and services Rick Steves and Europe Through the
Back Door offer you, ask us for our 64-page catalog.

Eurailpasses . . .

...cost the same everywhere. We carefully examine each
order and include for no extra charge a 90-minute Rick
Steves VHS video Train User's Guide, helpful itinerary
advice, Eurail train schedule booklet and map, plus a free
22 Days book of your choice! Send us a check for the cost
of the pass(es) you want along with your legal name (as it
appears on your passport), a proposed itinerary (including
dates and places of entry and exit if known), choice of 22 Days book
(Europe, Brit, Spain/Port, Scand, France, or Germ/Switz/Aust) and a list of
questions. Within 2 weeks of receiving your order we'll send you your
pass(es) and any other information pertinent to your trip. Due to this unique service Rick Steves sells more passes than anyone on the West Coast
and you'll have an efficient and expertly-organized Eurail trip.

Back Door Tours

We encourage independent travel, but for those who want
a tour in the Back Door style, we do offer a 22-day "Best of
Europe" tour. For complete details, send for our free 32
page tour booklet.

*All orders will be processed within 2 weeks and include tax (where applicable),
shipping and a one year's subscription to our Back Door Travel newsletter.
Prices good through 1992. Sorry, no credit cards. Send checks to:*

Europe Through The Back Door ● 120 Fourth Ave. N.
Box C-2009 ● Edmonds, WA 98020 ● (206) 771-8303

Other Books from John Muir Publications

Adventure Vacations: From Trekking in New Guinea to Swimming in Siberia, Richard Bangs (65-76-9) 256 pp. $17.95

Asia Through the Back Door, 3rd ed., Rick Steves and John Gottberg (65-48-3) 326 pp. $15.95

Being a Father: Family, Work, and Self, *Mothering* Magazine (65-69-6) 176 pp. $12.95

Buddhist America: Centers, Retreats, Practices, Don Morreale (28-94-X) 400 pp. $12.95

Bus Touring: Charter Vacations, U.S.A., Stuart Warren with Douglas Bloch (28-95-8) 168 pp. $9.95

California Public Gardens: A Visitor's Guide, Eric Sigg (65-56-4) 304 pp. $16.95

Catholic America: Self-Renewal Centers and Retreats, Patricia Christian-Meyer (65-20-3) 325 pp. $13.95

Complete Guide to Bed & Breakfasts, Inns & Guesthouses, 1991-92, Pamela Lanier (65-43-2) 520 pp. $16.95

Costa Rica: A Natural Destination, Ree Strange Sheck (65-51-3) 280 pp. $15.95

Elderhostels: The Students' Choice, Mildred Hyman (65-28-9) 224 pp. $12.95 (2nd ed. available 5/91 $15.95)

Environmental Vacations: Volunteer Projects to Save the Planet, Stephanie Ocko (65-78-5) 240 pp. $15.95

Europe 101: History & Art for the Traveler, 4th ed., Rick Steves and Gene Openshaw (65-79-3) 372 pp. $15.95

Europe Through the Back Door, 9th ed., Rick Steves (65-42-4) 432 pp. $16.95

Floating Vacations: River, Lake, and Ocean Adventures, Michael White (65-32-7) 256 pp. $17.95

Gypsying After 40: A Guide to Adventure and Self-Discovery, Bob Harris (28-71-0) 264 pp. $14.95

The Heart of Jerusalem, Arlynn Nellhaus (28-79-6) 336 pp. $12.95

Indian America: A Traveler's Companion, Eagle/Walking Turtle (65-29-7) 424 pp. $16.95 (2nd ed. available 7/91 $16.95)

Mona Winks: Self-Guided Tours of Europe's Top Museums, Rick Steves and Gene Openshaw (28-85-0) 456 pp. $14.95

Opera! The Guide to Western Europe's Great Houses, Karyl Lynn Zietz (65-81-5) 280 pp. $18.95 (Available 4/91)

Paintbrushes and Pistols: How the Taos Artists Sold the West, Sherry C. Taggett and Ted Schwarz (65-65-3) 280 pp. $17.95

The People's Guide to Mexico, 8th ed., Carl Franz (65-60-2) 608 pp. $17.95

The People's Guide to RV Camping in Mexico, Carl Franz with Steve Rogers (28-91-5) 320 pp. $13.95

Preconception: A Woman's Guide to Preparing for Pregnancy and Parenthood, Brenda E. Aikey-Keller (65-44-0) 232 pp. $14.95

Ranch Vacations: The Complete Guide to Guest and Resort, Fly-Fishing, and Cross-Country Skiing Ranches, Eugene Kilgore (65-30-0) 392 pp. $18.95 (2nd ed. available 5/91 $18.95)

Schooling at Home: Parents, Kids, and Learning, *Mothering* Magazine (65-52-1) 264 pp. $14.95

The Shopper's Guide to Art and Crafts in the Hawaiian Islands, Arnold Schuchter (65-61-0) 272 pp. $13.95

The Shopper's Guide to Mexico, Steve Rogers and Tina Rosa (28-90-7) 224 pp. $9.95

Ski Tech's Guide to Equipment, Skiwear, and Accessories, edited by Bill Tanler (65-45-9) 144 pp. $11.95

Ski Tech's Guide to Maintenance and Repair, edited by Bill Tanler (65-46-7) 160 pp. $11.95

Teens: A Fresh Look, *Mothering* Magazine (65-54-8) 240 pp. $14.95

A Traveler's Guide to Asian Culture, Kevin Chambers (65-14-9) 224 pp. $13.95

Traveler's Guide to Healing Centers and Retreats in North America, Martine Rudee and Jonathan Blease (65-15-7) 240 pp. $11.95

Understanding Europeans, Stuart Miller (65-77-7) 272 pp. $14.95
Undiscovered Islands of the Caribbean, 2nd ed., Burl Willes (65-55-6) 232 pp. $14.95
Undiscovered Islands of the Mediterranean, Linda Lancione Moyer and Burl Willes (65-53-X) 232 pp. $14.95
A Viewer's Guide to Art: A Glossary of Gods, People, and Creatures, Marvin S. Shaw and Richard Warren (65-66-1) 152 pp. $10.95

2 to 22 Days Series
These pocket-size itineraries (4½″ × 8″) are a refreshing departure from ordinary guidebooks. Each offers 22 flexible daily itineraries that can be used to get the most out of vacations of any length. Included are not only "must see" attractions but also little-known villages and hidden "jewels" as well as valuable general information.
22 Days Around the World, Roger Rapoport and Burl Willes (65-31-9) 200 pp. $9.95 (1992 ed. available 8/91 $11.95)
2 to 22 Days Around the Great Lakes, 1991 ed., Arnold Schuchter (65-62-9) 176 pp. $9.95
22 Days in Alaska, Pamela Lanier (28-68-0) 128 pp. $7.95
22 Days in the American Southwest, 2nd ed., Richard Harris (28-88-5) 176 pp. $9.95
22 Days in Asia, Roger Rapoport and Burl Willes (65-17-3) 136 pp. $7.95 (1992 ed. available 8/91 $9.95)
22 Days in Australia, 3rd ed., John Gottberg (65-40-8) 148 pp. $7.95 (1992 ed. available 8/91 $9.95)
22 Days in California, 2nd ed., Roger Rapoport (65-64-5) 176 pp. $9.95
22 Days in China, Gaylon Duke and Zenia Victor (28-72-9) 144 pp. $7.95
22 Days in Europe, 5th ed., Rick Steves (65-63-7) 192 pp. $9.95
22 Days in Florida, Richard Harris (65-27-0) 136 pp. $7.95 (1992 ed. available 8/91 $9.95)
✒ **22 Days in France,** Rick Steves (65-07-6) 154 pp. $7.95 (1991 ed. available 4/91 $9.95)
22 Days in Germany, Austria & Switzerland, 3rd ed., Rick Steves (65-39-4) 136 pp. $7.95
22 Days in Great Britain, 3rd ed., Rick Steves (65-38-6) 144 pp. $7.95 (1991 ed. available 4/91 $9.95)
22 Days in Hawaii, 2nd ed., Arnold Schuchter (65-50-5) 144 pp. $7.95 (1992 ed. available 8/91 $9.95)
22 Days in India, Anurag Mathur (28-87-7) 136 pp. $7.95
22 Days in Japan, David Old (28-73-7) 136 pp. $7.95
22 Days in Mexico, 2nd ed., Steve Rogers and Tina Rosa (65-41-6) 128 pp. $7.95
22 Days in New England, Anne Wright (28-96-6) 128 pp. $7.95 (1991 ed. available 4/91 $9.95)
2 to 22 Days in New Zealand, 1991 ed., Arnold Schuchter (65-58-0) 176 pp. $9.95
22 Days in Norway, Sweden, & Denmark, Rick Steves (28-83-4) 136 pp. $7.95 (1991 ed. available 4/91 $9.95)
22 Days in the Pacific Northwest, Richard Harris (28-97-4) 136 pp. $7.95 (1991 ed. available 4/91 $9.95)
22 Days in the Rockies, Roger Rapoport (65-68-8) 176 pp. $9.95
22 Days in Spain & Portugal, 3rd ed., Rick Steves (65-06-8) 136 pp. $7.95
22 Days in Texas, Richard Harris (65-47-5) 176 pp. $9.05
22 Days in Thailand, Derk Richardson (65-57-2) 176 pp. $9.95
22 Days in the West Indies, Cyndy Morreale and Sam Morreale (28-74-5)136 pp. $7.95

"Kidding Around" Travel Guides for Young Readers
Written for kids eight years of age and older. Generously illustrated in two colors with imaginative characters and images. An adventure to read and a treasure to keep.
Kidding Around Atlanta, Anne Pedersen (65-35-1) 64 pp. $9.95
Kidding Around Boston, Helen Byers (65-36-X) 64 pp. $9.95
Kidding Around Chicago, Lauren Davis (65-70-X) 64 pp. $9.95
Kidding Around the Hawaiian Islands, Sarah Lovett (65-37-8) 64 pp. $9.95
Kidding Around London, Sarah Lovett (65-24-6) 64 pp. $9.95
Kidding Around Los Angeles, Judy Cash (65-34-3) 64 pp. $9.95

Kidding Around the National Parks of the Southwest, Sarah Lovett 108 pp. $12.95

Kidding Around New York City, Sarah Lovett (65-33-5) 64 pp. $9.95

Kidding Around Paris, Rebecca Clay (65-82-3) 64 pp. $9.95 (Available 4/91)

Kidding Around Philadelphia, Rebecca Clay (65-71-8) 64 pp. $9.95

Kidding Around San Francisco, Rosemary Zibart (65-23-8) 64 pp. $9.95

Kidding Around Santa Fe, Susan York (65-99-8) 64 pp. $9.95 (Available 5/91)

Kidding Around Seattle, Rick Steves (65-84-X) 64 pp. $9.95 (Available 4/91)

Kidding Around Washington, D.C., Anne Pedersen (65-25-4) 64 pp. $9.95

Environmental Books for Young Readers

Written for kids eight years and older. Examines the environmental issues and opportunities that today's kids will face during their lives.

The Indian Way: Learning to Communicate with Mother Earth, Gary McLain (65-73-4) 114 pp. $9.95

The Kids' Environment Book: What's Awry and Why, Anne Pedersen (55-74-2) 192 pp. $13.95

No Vacancy: The Kids' Guide to Population and the Environment, Glenna Boyd (61-000-7) 64 pp. $9.95 (Available 8/91)

Rads, Ergs, and Cheeseburgers: The Kids' Guide to Energy and the Environment, Bill Yanda (65-75-0) 108 pp. $12.95

''Extremely Weird'' Series for Young Readers

Written for kids eight years of age and older. Designed to help kids appreciate the world around them. Each book includes full-color photographs with detailed and entertaining descriptions.

Extremely Weird Bats, Sarah Lovett (61-008-2) 48 pp. $9.95 paper (Available 6/91)

Extremely Weird Frogs, Sarah Lovett (61-006-6) 48 pp. $9.95 paper (Available 6/91)

Extremely Weird Spiders, Sarah Lovett (61-007-4) 48 pp. $9.95 paper (Available 6/91)

Automotive Repair Manuals

How to Keep Your VW Alive, 14th ed., (65-80-7) 440 pp. $19.95

How to Keep Your Subaru Alive (65-11-4) 480 pp. $19.95

How to Keep Your Toyota Pickup Alive (28-81-3) 392 pp. $19.95

How to Keep Your Datsun/Nissan Alive (28-65-6) 544 pp. $19.95

Other Automotive Books

The Greaseless Guide to Car Care Confidence: Take the Terror Out of Talking to Your Mechanic, Mary Jackson (65-19-X) 224 pp. $14.95

Off-Road Emergency Repair & Survival, James Ristow (65-26-2) 160 pp. $9.95

Ordering Information

If you cannot find our books in your local bookstore, you can order directly from us. Please check the ''Available'' date above. If you send us money for a book not yet available, we will hold your money until we can ship you the book. Your books will be sent to you via UPS (for U.S. destinations). UPS will not deliver to a P.O. Box; please give us a street address. Include $2.75 for the first item ordered and $.50 for each additional item to cover shipping and handling costs. For airmail within the U.S., enclose $4.00. All foreign orders will be shipped surface rate; please enclose $3.00 for the first item and $1.00 for each additional item. Please inquire about foreign airmail rates.

Method of Payment

Your order may be paid by check, money order, or credit card. We cannot be responsible for cash sent through the mail. All payments must be made in U.S. dollars drawn on a U.S. bank. Canadian postal money orders in U.S. dollars are acceptable. For VISA, MasterCard, or American Express orders, include your card number, expiration date, and your signature, or call (800) 888-7504. Books ordered on American Express cards can be shipped only to the billing address of the cardholder. Sorry, no C.O.D.'s. Residents of sunny New Mexico, add 5.875% tax to the total.

Address all orders and inquiries to:

John Muir Publications
P.O. Box 613
Santa Fe, NM 87504
(505) 982-4078
(800) 888-7504